# The Mission of the Holy Spirit

Written by
Wade C. Graber

Innovo
Publishing

Published by
Innovo Publishing LLC
www.innovopublishing.com
1-888-546-2111

Innovo
Publishing

Providing Full-Service Publishing Services for
Christian Authors, Artists & Organizations: Hardbacks, Paperbacks,
eBooks, Audiobooks, Music & Videos

**THE MISSION OF THE HOLY SPIRIT**

ISBN 13: 978-1-936076-51-2
ISBN 10: 1-936076-51-9

Cover Design & Interior Layout: Innovo Publishing LLC

Printed in the United States of America
U.S. Printing History

First Edition: December 2010

# Table of Contents

# Introduction

Y ou are the mission of the Holy Spirit! The Holy Spirit is on a mission and you are it! You are the mission or mission field of God the Holy Spirit! ". . . you are God's field" (I Corinthians 3:9). He wants to do a multitude of ministries in your life! Ultimately, He wants to indwell you and transform you into the image of the Lord Jesus Christ. The Holy Spirit is a missionary. You are His mission. He desires to instill Christ-likeness in your life.

Remember, God exists as Father, Son, and Holy Spirit—God the Father, God the Son, and God the Holy Spirit. "God is Spirit, and those who worship Him, must worship in spirit and truth" (John 4:24). When we speak of the Holy Spirit, we are referring to God.

The purpose of this book is to give some perspective on the awesome numerous facets of ministry that the Holy Spirit wants to perform in your life. The list in this book is by no means exhaustive. I initially discovered 126 ministries or actions of the Holy Spirit as recorded in the New Testament. The non-exhaustive list of missions of the Holy Spirit recorded in this book was determined by grouping synonyms and expressing multiple definitions of original Greek concepts (i.e. paraclete may mean comforter, helper, or encourager). Also, some verses speak of more than one facet of the mission of the Spirit. A reference may be used multiple times or only for its primary use in a particular verse. Certainly, the groupings of concepts and variations of the Greek words could be organized in different ways, but I pray that the message and ministry of the Spirit are not lost in debating diverse combinations. The eternal Spirit will endlessly point us to Jesus who is eternal. God the Holy Spirit will never run out of ways to do ministry and mission in your life.

Remember, the length of the chapter does not express importance or priority of a particular mission no more than the Minor Prophets are less important because of the length of their writings. No matter the mission or the length of the writing, I challenge you to think about and meditate on each mission before you read the next mission of the Spirit. This book is not meant to be a "quick read." It is information to ponder and contemplate to see if the Holy Spirit is ministering a particular mission to you.

I encourage and challenge you to be yielded and surrendered to the Holy Spirit as He comes to do His missionary work in your heart and life.

Think on these things. Meditate.

# Mission 1: Abide in You

Y ou are the mission of the Holy Spirit! The Holy Spirit is on a mission and you are it! You are the mission field of God the Holy Spirit! He wants to get to you and get into you before the enemy occupies you. God the Holy Spirit wants to abide in you, indwell you, and possess you.

When you were conceived, you became a potential residence for spiritual beings. It is vital to keep the enemy or demonic spirit out of you until the Holy Spirit occupies you. Until you are indwelt or possessed by God the Holy Spirit, you are vacant territory for any spirit to indwell you. The "Vacancy" sign of your spirit is lit up until you are indwelt by some spirit. Pray that the Holy Spirit is the first one to move into you by a heart-motivated invitation. It is the same for infants, children, youth, and adults, so pray to God that no other spirit enters your babies or you!

When is it possible for an individual to be possessed by a demonic spirit or indwelt by the Holy Spirit? Is there a particular time or age when indwelling or possessing can occur? To my knowledge, there is not a specifically designated chronological moment when indwelling happens in an individual. The Bible gives us examples of infants and children who become either indwelt by the Spirit or possessed by a demon.

On the positive side of indwelling, Jesus was conceived by the Holy Spirit (Matthew 1:18, 20). Mary's pregnancy with Jesus was a one-of-a-kind, extraordinary, unique, and divine conception. The presence and power of the Holy Spirit in Mary's womb was exclusive and greater than any other pregnancy. Jesus, including His time spent in the womb, was greater than everyone, even John the Baptist. John was, ". . . filled with the Holy Spirit, even from his mother's womb" (Luke 1:15). God can sovereignly indwell an infant in or out of the womb, "For with God nothing will be impossible" (Luke 1:37).

On the negative side of indwelling or possession, we have a few biblical possibilities. Matthew 17:18 records Jesus casting out a demon from an epileptic child (Greek—*pais*).[1] Mark 7:25–30 is the record of Jesus casting out an unclean spirit/demon from a woman's little daughter (vs. 25, Greek—*thugatrion*)[2] who was also a child (vs. 30, Greek—*paidion*).[3] English definitions of the Greek words used for *child* on these two occasions include infant and child. An infant or child was demon possessed/indwelt and Jesus exorcised the evil spirit. We don't know the specific age of either child, but conceptually we know that they were very young. We do know that God the Holy Spirit wants to be your exclusive Indweller.

One of the most powerful uses of a conjunction in the entire Bible can be found in John 14:17 where we see the tiny word "but" carrying with it some of the greatest spiritual ramifications of all times. The same dynamic can be said of the prepositional change from "with" to "in" as recorded in the same verse. The entire sentence reads like this:

*And I will pray the Father, and He will give you another Helper, that He may abide with you forever, even the Spirit of truth, whom the world cannot receive, because it neither sees Him nor knows Him;* **but** *you know Him, for He dwells* **with** *you and will be* **in** *you (John 14:16–17).*

The external presence and ministry of the Holy Spirit would be changed to an internal abiding presence. The Spirit would move into believers and take up residence within them. Twice (I Corinthians. 3:16, 6:19) Paul asked the Corinthians if they knew that their bodies were the temple/dwelling place of God the Holy Spirit. Romans 8:9 reminds us that believers are indwelt and it is impossible to be saved and not be possessed by the Holy Spirit. If we do not have the Spirit in us, then we do not belong to Christ. (Jude 1:19 tells us that the false teachers do not have the Spirit). In Romans 8:11, Paul goes on to tell us that the same Spirit that raised Christ from the dead dwells in believers! Wow!

Christians/believers/disciples/children of God are indwelt! Where did God send the Holy Spirit when you became His child? "And because you are sons, God has sent forth the Spirit of His Son into your hearts, crying out, 'Abba, Father!'" (Galatians 4:6). He comes to live in our innermost being, our hearts, just like the prophet Ezekiel foretold:

*I will give you a new heart and put a new spirit within you; I will take the heart of stone out of your flesh and give you a heart of flesh. I will put My Spirit within you and cause you to walk in My statutes, and you will keep My judgments and do them (Ezekiel 36:26–27).*

James wants the readers to determine if the scripture is vain when he speaks of the desires of the Spirit and states, "The Spirit who dwells in us yearns jealously (James 4:5)." God craves an exclusive love relationship with you. He desires an adultery-free union with you. The Spirit is passionate for deep intimacy with you. There is not a closer more intimate reality than being in someone or having someone in you. Internal presence and motivation compel the Holy Spirit to zealously guard His relationship with you.

John wrote these words concerning indwelling:

*Now he who keeps His commandments abides in Him, and He in him. And by this we know that He abides in us, by the Spirit whom He has given us. . . . By this we know that we abide in Him, and He in us, because He has given us of His Spirit (I John 3:24, 4:13).*

Abiding is confirmed by obedience to God's commands and the indwelling of the Holy Spirit. If the Holy Spirit is in us, then we should know it. We know when a tiny sticker is in our skin. We know when we have food in our mouths or somewhere in our digestive tract. We know that we have a beating heart inside of our body by laying a hand on our chest or feeling our pulse. We should know when the Spirit of the Creator of the universe indwells us. We should know that we have an enduring, unending relationship with God because we are the permanent living quarters of the Spirit. He is alive and He is in us! Wow!

Receive Him! Jesus breathed on His disciples and said, "Receive the Holy Spirit" (John 20:22). Peter said, "Repent and let every one of you be baptized in the name of Jesus Christ for the remission of sins; and you shall receive the gift of the Holy Spirit" (Acts 2:38). John and Peter went from Jerusalem to Samaria to pray for the new believers, ". . . that they might receive the Holy Spirit . . . Then they laid hands on them, and they received the Holy Spirit" (Acts 8:15b, 17). When the Gentiles responded to the preaching of Peter and the giving of the Holy Spirit, Peter asked, "Can anyone forbid water, that these should not be baptized who have received the Holy Spirit just as we have?" (Acts 10:47). Paul asked the disciples in Ephesus, "Did you receive the Holy Spirit when you believed?" (Acts 19:2a). The early church was concerned that new believers realized that they had received the Holy Spirit. They were now indwelt by God the Holy Spirit.

The Spirit was given to be received by believers as a blessing and benefit to life. The indwelling Spirit is not for bondage and fear, but for the reality of spiritual adoption (Romans 8:15). The Holy Spirit received from God is to help us, ". . . know the things that have been freely given to us by God" (I Corinthians 2:12b). God the Holy Spirit is received by faith and not by works (Galatians 3:2). Receive Him! Let Him into the home of your heart as an eternal resident.

You are the mission of the Holy Spirit! The Holy Spirit is on a mission and you are it! You are the mission field of God the Holy Spirit! He wants to abide in you, indwell you, possess you.

Think on these things. Meditate.

# *Mission 2: Access You*

Y ou are the mission of the Holy Spirit! The Holy Spirit is on a mission and you are it! You are the mission field of God the Holy Spirit! He wants to give you access to His presence and grace.

God the Holy Spirit is identified in Hebrews 10:29 as the "Spirit of grace." God's grace makes all things possible in the life of the believer. "The Holy Spirit is God's grace personified within the believer."[4] It is by the Spirit of grace that we are indwelt, affirmed, anointed, baptized, built up, comforted, commissioned, communed with, convicted, empowered, filled, gifted, led, inspired, justified, prospered, rebirthed, released, renewed, resurrected, sanctified, secured, strengthened, instructed, transformed, and unified.

Access to God the Father was made possible by the Holy Spirit through the blood sacrifice of Jesus Christ. "For through Him we both have access by one Spirit to the Father" (Ephesians 2:18). Jews and Gentiles are to be united into oneness and peace through the slaying of Jesus on the cross. The crucifixion dynamics acknowledged by faith pave the way for the Spirit of grace to provide access to the Father for us. Paul wrote it like this to the Romans:

> *Therefore, having been justified by faith, we have peace with God through our Lord Jesus Christ, through whom also we have access by faith into this grace in which we stand, and rejoice in hope of the glory of God (Romans 5:1–2).*

The visual spiritual expression of this access is recorded in all three of the Synoptic Gospels. The background for this event and illustration is found in Exodus 26 in the description of the tabernacle:

> *You shall make a veil woven of blue and purple and scarlet yarn, and fine linen thread. It will be woven with an artistic design of cherubim (Exodus 26:31).*

Ryrie reminds us of some basic information about this special veil. He writes:

> The inner veil separated the Holy Place (which contained the Altar of Incense, the lampstand, and the table for the bread) from the Holy of Holies (which contained the Ark and the Mercy Seat). Josephus reported that the veil was four inches thick, was renewed every year, and that horses tied to each side could not pull it apart. It barred all but the High Priest from the presence of God, but when it was torn in two at the death of Jesus of Nazareth (see Mark 15:38), access to God was made available to all who come through Him.[5]

When Jesus died on the cross, "the veil of the temple was torn in two from top to bottom" (Mark 15:38). One result of the crucifixion of Jesus was access. Now, not just the high priest, but any believer can come to God and enter the Holy of Holies by the access of the Spirit. Paul wrote:

> But now in Christ Jesus you who once were far off have been made near by the blood of Christ. For He Himself is our peace, who has made both one, and has broken down the middle wall of division between us, having abolished in His flesh the enmity, that is, the law of commandments contained in ordinances, so as to create in Himself one new man from two, thus making peace, and that He might reconcile them both to God in one body through the cross, thereby putting to death the enmity. And He came and preached peace to you who were afar off and to those who were near. For through Him we both have access by one Spirit to the Father (Ephesians 2:13–18).

People lock their keys in their vehicles all of the time. Access into the vehicle is the door or window. The best option to enter the vehicle is the key to unlock the door. Over the years, people have accessed the interior of their locked cars with duplicate keys, police, road assistance businesses, a locksmith, a clothes hanger, a flat tool for that purpose, a rock, or other window-breaking utensils. On a Judson Church youth tour, when they were locked out of the bus, the kids slid the skinniest boy through the school bus window. He removed the board that blocked the walk-in door from the inside, and all of the youth were able to enter the bus. Before Jesus' sacrifice for us, only the high priest could enter the inner room of the tabernacle one time a year and make a blood offering. The limitation of access because of the sacrificial system of the law is found in Hebrews 9:8, ". . . the Holy Spirit indicating this, that the way into the Holiest of All was not yet made manifest while the first tabernacle was still standing." But when Jesus sacrificed His life for us on the cross, the Hebrew author continued the discussion:

> Therefore, brethren, having boldness to enter the Holiest by the blood of Jesus, by a new and living way which He consecrated for us, through the veil, that is, His flesh (Hebrews 10:19–20).

We can now enter the Holy of Holies because the blood has been shed, the veil has been torn, and the Door has been opened by the Spirit to access the Father. Jesus is the "Door" (John 10:1–9) and the Spirit is the Key.

You are the mission of the Holy Spirit! The Holy Spirit is on a mission and you are it! You are the mission field of God the Holy Spirit! Part of the mission of the Holy Spirit is to take us from faith in Jesus at the cross to the wonders of the Father in the throne room. The Spirit wants to give you access to God's grace and presence. God the Holy Spirit is on a mission to give you access to the Holy of Holies.

Think on these things. Meditate.

# Mission 3: Affirm To and Through You

Y ou are the mission of the Holy Spirit! The Holy Spirit is on a mission and you are it! You are the mission field of God the Holy Spirit! He wants to affirm you, give evidence of who He is, and demonstrate the reality of your relationship with Him.

The Holy Spirit affirmed the person and work of Jesus Christ while He was living on the earth. The three Synoptic Gospels all record the Holy Spirit descending upon Jesus like a dove at His baptism (Matthew 3:16; Mark 1:10; Luke 3:22). John's gospel also records the account of the descending Spirit (John 1:32), but he expounds on the event with these words:

> *I did not know Him, but He who sent me to baptize with water said to me, "Upon whom you see the Spirit descending, and remaining on Him, this is He who baptizes with the Holy Spirit. And I have seen and testified that this is the Son of God" (John 1:33–34).*

God the Holy Spirit confirmed that Jesus was the Son of God, the Messiah, God's Anointed One. The Spirit also affirmed that Jesus was the One who would baptize with the Holy Spirit.

We see other affirmations by the Holy Spirit of Jesus' essential being and ministry as we read the New Testament. An example is found in Matthew 12:28 in Christ's words, "But if I cast out demons by the Spirit of God, surely the kingdom of God has come upon you." Jesus points to the Holy Spirit as the One by whom He casts out demons. The Lord makes clear that exorcisms by the Spirit are evidences that the kingdom of God has arrived.

The early New Testament believers encountered the Spirit of God in a new way on the day of Pentecost. The sound was like a mighty rushing wind (Acts 2:2). The sight was tongues of fire (Acts 2:3). The speaking in tongues was confirmation that it was the arrival of the Holy Spirit in the New Covenant way. The Spirit attested to His entry by the diverse languages. Peter affirmed the message of the Spirit by declaring the fulfillment of the prophet Joel (Acts 2:16–21). The Spirit-inspired prophet said there would be a specific outpouring of the Holy Spirit and the Spirit-inspired apostle confirmed His arrival.

Since the Holy Spirit affirmed, gave evidence, and demonstrated His reality in Jesus and the early church, it is no surprise that He continues to be on that same mission. He wants to confirm that you belong to Him. He desires to affirm you as a child of God. The Spirit is passionate about being in a personal relationship with you and demonstrating the reality of that union. He can do that through the scriptures He inspired, divine interventions, spiritual victories, or any other way He sovereignly chooses to make Himself real and personal to you. You are His and He is yours.

You are the mission of the Holy Spirit! The Holy Spirit is on a mission and you are it! You are the mission field of God the Holy Spirit! He wants to affirm you, evidence Himself, and demonstrate the realities of His relationship with you.

Think on these things. Meditate.

# Mission 4: Anoint You

Y ou are the mission of the Holy Spirit! The Holy Spirit is on a mission and you are
it! You are the mission field of God the Holy Spirit! He wants to anoint you.

The anointing of the Holy Spirit is referred to in the New Testament with a
variety of terms: anoint, descend, fall on, come upon, pour out, send, give, baptize, send
forth, supply, etc. The external anointing concepts are used like the Old Testament
dynamics for most of the New Testament record. The Holy Spirit is seen like a dove
"descending" and "alighting" upon Jesus at His water baptism (Matthew 3:16). The
prophecy of Isaiah 42:1–4 recorded in Matthew 12:18–21 includes the foretelling words,
"I will put My Spirit upon Him." The same phraseology is used in the Isaiah 61:1–2
prophecy that Luke records in 4:18–19:

> The Spirit of the Lord God is upon Me, because He has anointed Me to
> preach good tidings to the poor; He has sent me to heal the brokenhearted, To
> proclaim liberty to the captives, And the opening of the prison to those who are bound;
> To proclaim the acceptable year of the Lord, And the day of vengeance of our God; To
> comfort all who mourn (Isaiah 61:1–2).

The Old Covenant/Testament process of anointing externally for service or
position is seen in the Old and New Testament.  We also see another facet of
anointing introduced to us in Luke 11:13 and John 3:34. Jesus taught His disciples the
following lesson:

> If you then, being evil, know how to give good gifts to your children, how
> much more will your heavenly Father give the Holy Spirit to those who ask Him!
> (Luke 11:13).

The testimony of John the Baptist concerning Jesus refers to the
anointing/giving of the Holy Spirit in calculable yet limitless quantity: "For He whom
God has sent speaks the words of God, for God docs not give the Spirit by measure"
(John 3:34). The anointing/outpouring/giving/dispersal of the Holy Spirit is measurable
except in the portion given to Jesus the Christ—the Anointed of God.

Later, Paul communicates that the issue of the motive of preaching Christ will be
solved by two primary factors: intercessory prayer and the "supply of the Spirit of Jesus
Christ" (Philippians 1:19). Whatever the "calibration" or "amount" of the Spirit God has
for you, there is no question that He wants to anoint you for service and ministry.

We understand the anointing of the Holy Spirit more clearly when we discover
the external and the internal ramifications of Spirit anointing. I John 2:20 and 27 clarify
this spiritual blessing and mission of the Spirit:

*But you have an anointing from the Holy One, and you know all things . . . But the anointing which you have received from Him abides in you, and you do not need that anyone teach you; but as the same anointing teaches you concerning all things, and is true, and is not a lie, and just as it has taught you, you will abide in Him (I John 2:20,27).*

The anointing is the Holy Spirit Himself. He is the oil of God for your soul and spirit. He is the internal anointing that abides/lives in you. He is the anointing that can teach you directly without the necessity of a human instructor. He is the anointing that knows everything, so He can teach you all things. He is the anointing that is truth, so He teaches you what is true and never gives you false information. He is the anointing that teaches you truth, life, and how to abide in Him.

We become indwelt by God the Holy Spirit when we are born again. The Holy Spirit not only comes upon us externally for His purposes, but He anoints us internally with revelation, knowledge, teaching, and truth. This anointing will enable us to not be deceived, and we will continue to abide in Him.

You are the mission of the Holy Spirit! The Holy Spirit is on a mission and you are it! You are the mission field of God the Holy Spirit! He wants to anoint you with His oil of service, ministry, revelation, knowledge, teaching, and truth. After all, Jesus is the Christ, the Anointed One, and you are a Christian—an anointed one.

Think on these things. Meditate.

# Mission 5: Baptize You

Y ou are the mission of the Holy Spirit! The Holy Spirit is on a mission and you are it! You are the mission field of God the Holy Spirit! He wants to baptize you. He desires your spiritual immersion.

Holy Spirit baptism is interpreted in diverse ways. Even a secular dictionary is clear that "baptism" is a transliteration of the original Greek word *baptisma*, which means to dip or immerse.[6] The Holy Spirit is involved in an immersion that He craves for your life. It is an internal immersion.

John the Baptist foretold of Jesus, "He will baptize you with the Holy Spirit and fire" (Matthew 3:11). Jesus is the Baptizer. Unlike John who baptized with water, Jesus would immerse with the Holy Spirit.

In John 1:33, John the apostle's record of John the Baptist's testimony includes God's declaration, "Upon whom you see the Spirit descending and remaining on Him, this is He who baptizes with the Holy Spirit." Jesus is the "Immerser.".Again, unlike John, who baptized with water as God the Father commissioned, Jesus baptizes with the Spirit.

Acts 1:5 relates some of the last words of Jesus after His resurrection and before His ascension: ". . . for John truly baptized with water, but you shall be baptized with the Holy Spirit not many days from now." It is no secret that Jesus will be the Baptizer and He will immerse with the Holy Spirit and not water.

Acts 2 begins the accounts of the ascended Christ baptizing believers with the Holy Spirit. The first believers to be immersed with the Spirit experienced diverse, observable dynamics—rushing wind, fiery tongues, various known languages, intoxicated behavior, prophetic fulfillment, and empowered preaching. Repentant believers received the gift of the Holy Spirit from Jesus the Immerser. The same identical thing happened with the Gentiles at Cornelius' place (Acts 10:44–48). Peter rehearsed the event before the Jewish believers at Jerusalem:

> *And as I began to speak, the Holy Spirit fell upon them, as upon us at the beginning. Then I remembered the word of the Lord, how He said, "John indeed baptized with water, but you shall be baptized with the Holy Spirit" (Acts 11:15–16).*

Jesus, the Baptizer, immersed or poured out His Spirit into believers. He continues to baptize believers with the Holy Spirit.

> *For by one Spirit we were all baptized into one body—whether Jews or Greeks, whether slaves or free—and have all been made to drink into one Spirit (I Corinthians 12:13).*

Jesus, the "Immerser," baptizes with the Holy Spirit. God the Father said it would happen that way. Jesus said it would happen that way. John the Baptist confirmed the Father's message and affirmed this ministry of the Son.

You are the mission of the Holy Spirit! The Holy Spirit is on a mission and you are it! You are the mission field of God the Holy Spirit! He wants you to be immersed in Himself by Jesus. He wants you to be surrendered and yielded to the Lord Jesus, so that when He wants to enter you, He is welcomed and gloriously received. The Holy Spirit wants you immersed, totally saturated with Himself, so that all of your words, actions, and life are under His influence. He wants you to have an internal immersion.

Think on these things. Meditate.

# Mission 6: Build You

Y ou are the mission of the Holy Spirit! The Holy Spirit is on a mission and you are it! You are the mission field of God the Holy Spirit! The One who created you wants to continue construction on you. The Holy Spirit desires to build you up or edify you. His construction in your life includes personal building and joining you together with other believers.

Ephesians 2:19–22 gives some clear construction terms to relate this concept of spiritual building. Paul wrote this long sentence:

> *Now, therefore, you are no longer strangers and foreigners, but fellow citizens with the saints and members of the household of God, having been built on the foundation of the apostles and prophets, Jesus Christ Himself being the chief cornerstone, in whom the whole building, being joined together, grows into a holy temple in the Lord, in whom you also are being built together for a habitation of God in the Spirit (Ephesians 2:19–22).*

The foundation has been laid, the cornerstone is in place, the walls have been erected, the roof is constructed, and the habitat for the Holy Spirit is formed. It is not just a matter of stone and mortar.

Mission is not just what we do. It is what God does in us. When the church family in El Cerillo, Mexico was ready to start construction after eight years of persecution and opposition, they handed me the first block—the cornerstone. The interpreter spoke their message, "We want you to pray over this block and lay the first block." It was a pretty exciting privilege. I took that block, put some mortar down, laid it in place, and began to pray over it. I can tell you what I did, but I cannot relay to you how deeply the Holy Spirit touched me at that moment. The simple construction process of laying the cornerstone for that village *templo* was spiritually a major event. Mission is not just what we do, but mission is what God does in us. We need to realize that we are an open mission field—open to whatever God the Holy Spirit wants to do in us.

The spiritual construction is an ongoing process that God does in us temples not made with human hands (Acts 7:48 and 17:24). Hebrews 3:4–6 tells us that God is the builder of the house, we are the house, and Jesus is the head of the house. Peter recorded this message:

> *Coming to Him as to a living stone, rejected indeed by men, but chosen by God and precious, you also as living stones, are being built up a spiritual house, a holy priesthood, to offer up spiritual sacrifices acceptable to God through Jesus Christ (I Peter 2:4–5).*

A stone, by itself, is not a building. Internal construction and shaping of an individual stone is crucial for Christ-likeness and mission with other believers. The Holy Spirit wants to build in you personally and connect you corporately with other believers. He desires to do spiritual construction in you because you are His temple and dwelling place. He has a passion to build you together with other believers for a spiritual dwelling place for Himself. You must be willing and ready for spiritual construction, reconstruction, and remodeling if you are serious about surrendering to the Holy Spirit to build your life and your relationships in His Holy temple.

You are the mission of the Holy Spirit! The Holy Spirit is on a mission and you are it! You are the mission field of God the Holy Spirit! He wants to continue to edify you and do spiritual construction in your life.

Think on these things. Meditate.

# Mission 7: Comfort, Encourage, and Help You

You are the mission of the Holy Spirit! The Holy Spirit is on a mission and you are it! You are the mission field of God the Holy Spirit. He wants to comfort, encourage, and help you in all matters of life.

God (Father, Son, and Holy Spirit) is identified in the New Testament as the Comforter, the Encourager, the Helper—the *Paraclete*. The One called to our side is what paraclete means, as it is a combination of the Greek concepts *para* (beside) and *kaleo* (to call).[7] God the Father is recognized as the "God of all comfort" (II Corinthians 1:3b). God the Son claims to be a Helper/Comforter when He introduces the Consoler that would continue His ministry; even the Holy Spirit:

> *And I will pray the Father, and He will give you another Helper, that He may abide with you forever, even the Spirit of truth, whom the world cannot receive, because it neither sees Him, nor knows Him; but you know Him, for He dwells with you and will be in you*
> *(John 14:16–17).*

John shares more information about the comforting, encouraging, helping ministry of the Holy Spirit. Some of these paraclete ministries are found in other missions of the Holy Spirit highlighted in this book. The Gospel of John includes the following dynamics of the Paraclete Holy Spirit:

> *But the Helper, the Holy Spirit, whom the Father will send in My name, He will teach you all things, and bring to your remembrance all things that I said to you (John 14:26).*

> *But when the Helper comes, whom I shall send to you from the Father, even the Spirit of truth who proceeds from the Father, He will testify of Me (John 15:26).*

> *However, when He, the Spirit of truth has come, He will guide you into all truth; for He will not speak on His own authority, but whatever He hears He will speak; and He will tell you things to come. He will glorify Me, for He will take of what is Mine and declare it to you (John 16:13–14).*

The Paraclete will comfort, encourage, and help you by being with you, by dwelling in you, by teaching you, by recalling the sayings of Christ, by empowering you to testify to Jesus, by guiding you into truth, by enabling you to glorify Jesus, by telling you about future things, and by declaring the things of the Father and Son to you.

You are the mission of the Holy Spirit! The Holy Spirit is on a mission and you are it! You are the mission field of God the Holy Spirit! He wants to comfort, encourage, and help you. Do you want His comfort, encouragement, and help as much as He wants to give it to you?

Think on these things. Meditate.

# Mission 8: Commission You

You are the mission of the Holy Spirit! The Holy Spirit is on a mission and you are it! You are the mission field of God the Holy Spirit! He wants to commission you—send you out to do His work.

One of the frailties of the church, in many cases, is that we are in defense mode. We put on the full armor of God (maybe) and wait around for the enemy to attack. We forget that we have an offensive weapon—the sword of the Spirit, the Word of God. We are not intentional about striking an attack against our enemy. Paul identified our spiritual opponents who attack us and who we need to oppose:

> Put on the whole armor of God, that you may be able to stand against the wiles of the devil. For we do not wrestle against flesh and blood, but against principalities, against powers, against the rulers of the darkness of this age, against spiritual hosts of wickedness in the heavenly places (Ephesians 6:11–12).

The commissioning ministry of the Holy Spirit puts us on offense. Luke began the record in Acts by giving account of what Jesus did through the Holy Spirit after the Ascension—". . . until the day in which He was taken up, after He through the Holy Spirit had given commandments to the apostles whom He had chosen . . ."(Acts 1:2). One of these commands/commissions that Jesus gave by the Spirit, before the Ascension, to be lived out after the Ascension is found in Acts 1:8:

> But you shall receive power when the Holy Spirit has come upon you and you shall be witnesses to Me in Jerusalem, and in all Judea, and Samaria, and to the end of the earth (Acts 1:8).

The commissions Jesus gave in the flesh and those given through the Spirit are missions that the Holy Spirit wants to do in your life. He commands us to love, forgive, help, pray, and witness which can only be accomplished by the power of the Holy Spirit.

Another obvious commissioning of God the Holy Spirit is recorded in Acts 13. After Luke identified the place—Antioch—and some of the prophets and teachers by name, he wrote:

> As they ministered to the Lord and fasted, the Holy Spirit said, "Now separate to Me Barnabas and Saul for the work to which I have called them." Then, having fasted and prayed, and laid hands on them, they sent them away. So, being sent out by the Holy Spirit, they went down to Seleucia, and from there they sailed to Cypress (Acts 13:2–4).

The missionary journeys began when the Holy Spirit commissioned men from the church to go do the work He planned for them. The apostles (sent out ones) started functioning at a new level of apostolic ministry.

Another example of the Holy Spirit's commissioning is found in Acts 20:28 when Paul spoke to the Ephesian elders. His parting exhortations included these words:

> *Therefore take heed to yourselves and to all the flock, among which the Holy Spirit has made you overseers, to shepherd the church of God which He purchased with His own blood (Acts 20:28).*

The commission of the Holy Spirit is not only for individuals, but also for church leaders, church families, and the whole of His church. His directives are to witness, plant churches, and care for the members of the churches. He wants every member to obey His call wherever and however He leads.

You are the mission of the Holy Spirit! The Holy Spirit is on a mission and you are it! You are the mission field of God the Holy Spirit! He wants to continue to commission you and send you out as He wills for His purposes.

Think on these things. Meditate.

# *Mission 9: Commune with You*

Y ou are the mission of the Holy Spirit! The Holy Spirit is on a mission and you are
it! You are the mission field of God the Holy Spirit! He wants to commune with
you. He wants to enjoy fellowship with you.

Two passages from the New Testament surfaced when contemplating this part
of the Holy Spirit's mission. The first verse is II Corinthians13:14, "The grace of the
Lord Jesus Christ, and the love of God, and the communion of the Holy Spirit be with
you all. Amen." The second passage is Philippians 2:1–2 which says:

> *Therefore, if there is any consolation in Christ, if any comfort of love, if any
> fellowship of the Spirit, if any affection and mercy, fulfill my joy by being like-minded,
> having the same love, being of one accord, of one mind (Philippians 2:1–2).*

It is fascinating to note in the original Greek language that both texts have the
communion/fellowship of the Spirit in the genitive case.[8] This case shows possession. It
is not only a matter of communion with God the Holy Spirit; it is participating in His
fellowship. We have the privilege of experiencing the Spirit's communion. Like the unity
of the Spirit we will discuss later, the fellowship of the Spirit belongs to Him. It is His!

The fellowship of the Holy Spirit is the kind of communion that God the Father,
God the Son, and God the Holy Spirit share with each other. It is similar to the oneness
that Jesus prayed for us to enjoy with Him and the Father as recorded in John 17:

> *…that they may all be one, as You, Father, are in Me, and I in You; that
> they also may be one in Us, that the world may believe that    You sent Me. And
> the glory which You gave Me I have given them, that they may be one just as We are
> one; I in them, and You in Me; that they may be made perfect in one, and that the
> world may know that You have sent Me, and have loved them as You have loved Me
> (John17:21–23).*

The fellowship of the Spirit is a natural dynamic that happens when the Holy
Spirit is present. He indwells you, so it is normal to commune with Him at all times as
He emanates fellowship. We may enrich that fellowship, or we may resist that spiritual
camaraderie, but it is constantly available to us because He is in us.

I'm a "communer" when it comes to God. I enjoy the fellowship that comes
from His Spirit and my spirit being together. Some people are first and foremost readers,
or prayers, or studiers, or servers, or helpers, or worshipers, or some other priority or
preference for communing with God. Communion or fellowship with God the Holy
Spirit includes the preferences of prayer, reading, serving, and worshiping, but I simply
love His presence in me. I love His company. It is like being in a room with the one you
love and not needing to say or do anything but enjoy their presence. I enjoy knowing

that I am indwelt. I am thrilled when He makes His presence known more personally and powerfully than at other times. I delight in His constant, unchanging occupancy in my heart. Before my feet hit the floor in the morning, I commune with Him and surrender my life, my family, and others to Him by name. I can trust Him to go with me and them through the day and relish His promise, "I will never leave you nor forsake you" (Hebrews 13:5). It is very much like Jesus' offer of fellowship:

> *Behold, I stand at the door and knock. If anyone hears My voice and opens the door, I will come in to him and dine with him, and he with Me (Revelation 3:20).*

You invite Jesus or the Holy Spirit to come into you. He comes in as He has promised. He enters to have fellowship with you like sitting around the table eating food and enjoying conversation. It is like Robert Boyd Munger's booklet, "My Heart Christ's Home." He wants to live together within you.

You are the mission of the Holy Spirit! The Holy Spirit is on a mission and you are it! You are the mission field of God the Holy Spirit! He wants to commune with you every waking moment. The Spirit wants you to participate in His fellowship, which He makes available to you by indwelling you and initiating relationship with you.

Think on these things. Meditate.

# Mission 10: Convict You

Y ou are the mission of the Holy Spirit! The Holy Spirit is on a mission and you are it! You are the mission field of God the Holy Spirit! He wants to convict you before and after you become a Christian.

One part of the Spirit's mission is to convict you of "sin, righteousness, and judgment" (John 16:8). His quest prior to your salvation is not to condemn you for your sin and unbelief in Christ, but to convince you of your sin. The Spirit wants you to see your imperfection compared to Jesus' perfection, so you see your need for a Savior. Jesus said, "You shall be perfect, just as your Father in heaven is perfect" (Matthew 5:48). The Holy Spirit wants you to know in your heart that you have violated God at least once in your life. He wants you to understand that only one sin is enough to separate you from God for all eternity. Every one of us has fallen short of God's holy righteous character and standards. There is no sense in denying that we have sinned. John wrote:

> If we say that we have no sin, we deceive ourselves, and the truth is not in us.
> If we confess our sins, He is faithful and just to forgive us our sins and to cleanse us
> from all unrighteousness. If we say that we have not sinned, we make Him a liar, and
> His word is not in us (I John 1:8–10).

The Holy Spirit desires to convince you that your goodness is not good enough to please God or to spend eternity with Him. He wants you to admit that you are a sinner, confess your sins to God, and receive His forgiveness and cleansing. You have sinned and need a Savior—Jesus Christ. Unbelief in Jesus Christ as your personal Savior is an unforgivable sin.

The Spirit also wants to convict you of righteousness. He has a passion for you to be in a right relationship with God. He wants you to realize that you are unrighteous without Jesus Christ who validated and confirmed His righteousness by His resurrection and ascension. The Holy Spirit wants you to know that God is righteous, perfect, pure, and holy. You are unrighteous, imperfect, impure, and profane. According to the lists recorded in Romans 1:29–30, Romans 3:10–18, and I Corinthians 6:9–11, unrighteousness can include being wicked, coveting, envying, backbiting, gossip, being prideful, disobeying parents, not seeking God, doing our thing and not God's plan, not doing good, speaking deceitfully, cursing, bitterness, not fearing God, sexual immorality, idolatry, adultery, homosexuality, sodomy, drunkenness, and stealing. If you have participated in any of these or any other of a multitude of acts or lifestyles of sin, then you are unrighteous.

But, there is good news! There is possibility and promise for you to be delivered from any unrighteousness and to become righteous. The Spirit desires for you to "love righteousness and hate wickedness" (Psalm 45:7a). The Spirit wants to convince you that the sacrifice of Jesus on the cross is the only way for you to be righteous (right with God). "For He made Him who knew no sin to be sin for us, that we might become the righteousness of God in Him" (II Corinthians 5:21). God the Father made God the Son, Jesus, to be punished as a sinner, so we sinners could be treated as righteous ones. Jesus, the Righteous One, took our sins upon Himself and allowed His holy Father to sentence Him to the consequential death of sin. Jesus' crucifixion was the result of our sin. His resurrection and ascension are the results of His righteousness. You can trust Him who went from righteous, to sin, to righteous, for your transformation from sinner to righteous one. Receive Him and His righteousness.

God the Holy Spirit wants to convict you of judgment. You cannot afford to disregard the Spirit's conviction of God's judgment now and forever. "It is appointed for men to die once, but after this the judgment" (Hebrews 9:27). You have an inescapable appointment with death that you will keep, whether you want to or not. Immediately after your body dies, you will stand before God in judgment. In that moment, you will not want to rest on your own goodness to get you into heaven because you won't make it. God is the Judge with the final say about where you and everyone will spend eternity. He has already determined that the Devil, the Antichrist, the False Prophet, the demons, and every unbeliever will be cast into the lake of fire for eternal torment and judgment because they rejected Jesus and His righteousness for their personal salvation (Revelation 20:10–15).

The Holy Spirit wants to convict you and convince you of the reality of God's judgment. God will judge you according to the standard of His Son, ". . . in the day when God will judge the secrets of men by Jesus Christ, according to my gospel" (Romans 2:16). He will judge you according to the measure of Jesus Christ the Righteous and Perfect One. The cross is the sign post that sin and sinners are punished, and future eternal punishment is in store for all who do not turn from sin and trust Jesus to save them.

The purpose of the Spirit's mission to convict you of sin, judgment, and righteousness is to convince you to turn from your sin, receive Jesus' righteousness, and avoid God's eternal judgment. But, His convicting mission does not stop when you become a Christian. Believers should continue to be alert to the Spirit's conviction of sin, judgment, and righteousness. God the Holy Spirit will convince you that your thought, motive, or action is sinfully charged or a sin itself. He will tell you if your thought, motive, or action will please or displease the Ultimate Judge. The Holy Spirit will show you through His inspired Word, if you are living a righteous life or living in unrighteousness. He will continue to speak truth to your spirit and bear witness to your conscience about right and wrong.

You are the mission of the Holy Spirit! The Holy Spirit is on a mission and you are it! You are the mission field of God the Holy Spirit! He will convict you to live a life that is not marked by sin, prepared to meet God in judgment, and determined by the righteousness of Jesus Christ.

Think on these things. Meditate.

# Mission 11: Empower You

Y ou are the mission of the Holy Spirit! The Spirit is on a mission and you are it! You are the mission field of God the Holy Spirit! He wants to empower you. He wants to embolden you, enable you, preserve you, and fill you with greater spiritual dynamic.

Luke 4:14 says, "Then Jesus returned in the power of the Spirit to Galilee, and news of Him went out through all the surrounding region" (Luke 4:14). Prior to this notation of the Spirit's power in Jesus' life, we observe some extraordinary dynamics. Jesus was filled with the Holy Spirit and led by the Spirit (Luke 4:1). He fasted for forty days (Luke 4:2). He was directly and forcefully tempted by Satan with three diverse appeals, but He did not succumb to the temptations (Luke 4:3–13). It is safe to conclude that in being filled with the Spirit and led by the Spirit that Jesus was empowered to fast forty days and not give in to Satan's temptations. Jesus was given boldness to battle the Devil. He was enabled to overcome the enemy. Jesus was kept from sin and persevered through the trials.

Furthermore, Jesus continued in the power of the Spirit after His wilderness ordeal to embrace His ministry. He established His teaching ministry in the synagogues (Luke 4:15). This particular synagogue experience that Luke documents in his gospel account ties together the Spirit's empowering and Jesus' teaching and preaching ministry. It is in His hometown synagogue in Nazareth that Jesus declared He was the fulfillment of the Isaiah 61 prophecy:

> *The Spirit of the Lord is upon Me, because He has anointed Me to preach the gospel to the poor; He has sent Me to heal the broken-hearted, to proclaim liberty to the captives and recovery of sight to the blind, to set at liberty those who are oppressed; to proclaim the accept able year of the Lord (Luke 4:18–19).*

Jesus acknowledged that it was the Spirit's anointing that enabled Him to preach, heal, proclaim, liberate, restore sight, and fulfill the prophecies of Isaiah 61.

Peter was aware of the empowering ministry of the Spirit in Jesus' life. His message to Cornelius and his household included these words:

> *. . . how God anointed Jesus of Nazareth with the Holy Spirit and power, who went about doing good and healing all who were oppressed by the devil, for God was with Him (Acts 10:38).*

We need total reliance on the Holy Spirit and to realize that all ministry happens because of the Spirit's empowering. One example is testifying about Jesus Christ. The Holy Spirit will give you power to witness today just as Jesus promised His disciples centuries ago.

*But you shall receive power when the Holy Spirit has come upon you; and you shall be witnesses to Me in Jerusalem, and in all Judea and Samaria, and to the end of the earth (Acts1:8).*

The apostle Paul wrote of two dynamics of the Holy Spirit's empowering in Romans 15. Paul's wish for his readers was a desire to know and experience abundantly God's hope, "by the power of the Holy Spirit" (Romans 15:13). Second, Paul expressed that the miraculous events, "the mighty signs and wonders" manifested in his ministry were done "by the power of the Spirit of God" (Romans 15:19).

Generically, Jesus made this declaration about empowered ministry that would happen after He returned to His Father and the Spirit had arrived:

*Most assuredly, I say to you, he who believes in Me, the works that I do he will do also; and greater works than these he will do, because I go to my Father (John 14:12).*

You are the mission of the Holy Spirit! The Holy Spirit is on a mission and you are it! You are the mission field of God the Holy Spirit! He wants to empower and enable you to do greater works and be more spiritually dynamic than you are today.

Think on these things. Meditate.

# Mission 12: Fill You

Y ou are the mission of the Holy Spirit! The Holy Spirit is on a mission and you are it! You are the mission field of God the Holy Spirit! He wants to fill you.

The New Testament has numerous references to Spirit fullness and being filled. Being full of the Spirit is the ongoing state of the indwelt believer, while being filled is what is observable at a certain moment or occasion. It is observable when someone is full of the Holy Spirit or being Spirit-filled. In tangible terms, indwelling is putting fuel in the gas tank. Spirit fullness is when the tank is so full the automatic shut off clicks on the gas pump nozzle. And, being filled with the Spirit is when the gas tank overflows and squirts fuel. This mission focuses on the Spirit's passion for you to be full of Him and filled by Him.

There are some pre-Pentecost references to Spirit fullness and being filled with the Holy Spirit. First, in the John the Baptist story, we see references to Spirit filling three times in Luke chapter one. The prophecy of God via an angel included these words:

> *For he will be great in the sight of the Lord, and shall drink neither wine nor strong drink. He will also be filled with the Holy Spirit, even from his mother's womb (Luke 1:15).*

The baby would be filled with the Spirit from the day he was born. This is a sovereign act of God to cause one to be Spirit-filled without repentance, willful desire, or any spiritual dynamics on the recipient's part. God determined that John the Baptist would be filled with the Holy Spirit from his birth. John's life would be marked by Spirit fullness.

Second, Luke 1:41 records a time when John's mother was filled when her pregnant relative came to see her:

> *And it happened, when Elizabeth heard the greeting of Mary, that the babe leaped in her womb, and Elizabeth was filled with the Holy Spirit (Luke 1:41).*

When Jesus' mother, Mary, greeted John the Baptist's mother, the encounter resulted in Elizabeth being filled with the Spirit. The spiritual dynamics of this event stimulated Elizabeth to be filled and to prophesy (Luke 1:42–45). This triggered a prophecy from Mary (Luke 1:46–55) that we surmise is also a result of being filled with the Spirit.

Third, Luke 1:67 records the moment when John the Baptist's father, Zacharias, was filled with the Holy Spirit. Since he was mute for nine months because he did not believe the angel Gabriel's message, Zacharias had a lot to say. The Holy Spirit filled him, loosened his tongue, and Zacharias prophesied. Like his wife Elizabeth, he was divinely filled in the moment and spoke God's message.

Jesus was not only conceived by the Holy Spirit, but He was also full of the Spirit and filled with the Spirit. After the Holy Spirit descended on Him at His baptism, we read, "Then Jesus, being filled with the Holy Spirit, returned from the Jordan and was led by the Spirit into the wilderness . . ." (Luke 4:1).

Jesus' filling was preparation for a leading that involved extreme spiritual warfare. His Spirit filling equipped Him to get victory over the temptations of the enemy—the Devil himself. Zacharias, Elizabeth, and Mary were filled to prophesy in the moment. Jesus was filled to overcome His enemy and triumph over the trials and temptations set before Him.

The biblical concept of living water gives us some comprehension and visualization of being filled with the Holy Spirit. The prophecies of Jeremiah include these words:

> *For My people have committed two evils: They have forsaken Me, the fountain of living waters, and hewn themselves cisterns—broken cisterns that can hold no water (Jeremiah 2:13).*

> *O Lord the hope of Israel, all who forsake You shall be ashamed. Those who depart from Me shall be written in the earth, because they have forsaken the Lord, the fountain of living waters (Jeremiah 17:13).*

In both passages, God identified Himself as "the fountain of living waters." Jesus taught about the living water fountain in His dialogue with the woman at the well and during the Feast of Tabernacles or Booths. Look at what Jesus said to the Samaritan woman at Jacob's well recorded in John 4:

> *If you knew the gift of God, and who it is who says to you, 'Give Me a drink,' you would have asked Him, and He would have given you living water. . . . Whoever drinks of this water will thirst again, but whoever drinks of the water that I shall give him will never thirst. But the water that I shall give him will become in him a fountain of water springing up into everlasting life (John 4:10, 13, 14).*

Jesus is the Giver of living water, which will become a fountain spewing out of believers. The fountain of living water, the Lord Himself/His Spirit, is further explained by Jesus during His proclamation at the Jewish feast:

> *If anyone thirsts, let him come to Me and drink. He who believes in Me, as the Scripture has said, out of his heart will flow rivers of living water (John 7:37–38).*

Verse 39 is the interpretation of Jesus' words:

> *But this He spoke concerning the Spirit, whom those believing in Him would receive; for the Holy Spirit was not yet given, because Jesus was not yet glorified (John 7:39).*

God the Holy Spirit is identified as the living water that would become a fountain in believers after Jesus ascended to the Father and was glorified. The outpouring of the Holy Spirit, who is the Living Water, began in the New Covenant way at Pentecost and has continued from that time. The quoted phrase in the Joel 2:28–29 prophecy, "I will pour out My Spirit," is identified by Peter in Acts 2:17–18, after "they were all filled with the Holy Spirit" (Acts 2:4). At this initial filling and outpouring, the Spirit gave the believers words that could be identified in the language of all the listeners found in Jerusalem that day of Pentecost.

As the church grew and the Holy Spirit kept filling the believers, we were given more accounts of the fountain of living water springing up and out of them. Peter was filled again with the Holy Spirit and preached (Acts 4:8). While believers were praying together, "they were all filled with the Holy Spirit, and they spoke the word of God with boldness" (Acts 4:31). The seven men selected to serve the people were to be full of the Spirit as one of the qualifications (Acts 6:3, 5). Stephen, one of the seven chosen to serve, was given an opportunity to see into heaven, and in that Spirit-filled moment others observed that he was "full of the Holy Spirit"(Acts 7:55–56). Ananias was sent to Straight Street to pray for the blinded Saul of Tarsus with this message:

> *Brother Saul, the Lord Jesus, who appeared to you on the road as you came, has sent me that you may receive your sight and be filled with the Holy Spirit (Acts 9:17).*

Barnabas was recognized as a man "full of the Holy Spirit" (Acts 11:24). Paul, the converted Saul, was filled with the Holy Spirit to bind and blind the sorcerer Elymas (Acts 13:9). The response to persecution was "the disciples were filled with joy and with the Holy Spirit" (Acts 13:52).

The most clear and direct exhortation to be filled with the Holy Spirit is Ephesians 5:18, "And do not be drunk with wine, in which is dissipation; but be filled with the Spirit." The Greek verb for filled (*plarousthe*) is a present, imperative, passive, second person, plural form.[9] It is a command to presently and continually allow the Holy Spirit to fill you and every believer. It is commanded for us to be Spirit-filled. God sovereignly does the filling since He is the fountain of living water. Our part is to get empty so He can fill us. We need to unplug any clogged arteries of our spiritual heart that may be filled with sinful plaque so the fountain of the Spirit will fill us with living water.

You are the mission of the Holy Spirit! The Holy Spirit is on a mission and you are it! You are the mission field of God the Holy Spirit! He wants you to be known as being full of the Spirit. He wants you to be yielded and surrendered so He can fill you with Himself for whatever ministry He has at hand. Keep on being filled

Think on these things. Meditate.

# Mission 13: Fruit You

Y ou are the mission of the Holy Spirit! The Holy Spirit is on a mission and you are it! You are the mission field of God the Holy Spirit! He wants to "fruit" you. The Spirit desires the natural produce of His presence to come to fruition in you.

Galatians 5:22–23 are the most common verses that set forth the teaching of the spiritual fruit, "But the fruit of the Spirit is love, joy, peace, longsuffering, kindness, goodness, faithfulness, gentleness, self-control" (Galatians 5:22, 23a). Love, joy, peace, etc. are the normal dynamics when God the Holy Spirit is present. Since He indwells us, His mission includes planting the fruit of His presence in us that produces the Spirit's fruit in our lives. It is the Holy Spirit's fruit, not our fruit. He wants to grow it in and out of our lives.

Since the word "fruit" is in the singular, we begin to comprehend that there is one fruit with nine elements of produce. We could say that there is one fruit with nine slices, or to stay with the fluid New Testament references to the Holy Spirit (i.e. "living water") the fruit of the Spirit is like mixed fruit punch. All of the flavors make one fruit drink. The Holy Spirit wants all nine spiritual flavors of His fruit to fill you and pour out into your life as we "have been all made to drink into one Spirit" (I Corinthians 12:13b). Our lives should be marked by love, joy, peace, etc. because we are yielded to the Spirit who indwells us. The fruit of the Spirit naturally exists with Him, and is to be normal for us as He performs His missionary endeavor in us.

The parenthetical of Ephesians 5:9 teaches us that the Spirit's fruit has a contextual container in addition to a literal fruit jar—us. Paul wrote, ". . . for the fruit of the Spirit is in all goodness, righteousness, and truth" (Ephesians 5:9).

Spiritual fruit exists and is lived in an attitude and environment of goodness, righteousness, and truth. Our entire spiritual walk is to be in an atmosphere of these three dynamics. When the fruit of the Spirit is manifest in us, our lives will be marked by God's goodness, God's righteousness, and God's truth. This concept is similar to the spiritual elements of the kingdom that Paul wrote about, "For the kingdom of God is not food and drink, but righteousness and peace and joy in the Holy Spirit" (Romans 14:17). As kingdom living components are righteousness, peace, and joy, so the facets of spiritual fruit are lived in God's righteousness, goodness, and truth.

Since love is the primary slice/juice of the fruit of the Spirit, let us use it as an example of how the Holy Spirit wants to "fruit" you with all nine ingredients. We begin with some of the familiar teachings on the preeminence of love.

> *You shall love the Lord your God with all your heart, with all your soul, and with all your mind. This is the first and greatest command. And the second is like it: you shall love your neighbor as yourself. On these two commandments hang all the Law and the Prophets (Matthew 22:37–40).*

*For God so loved the world that He gave His only begotten Son, that whoever believes in Him should not perish but have everlasting life (John 3:16).*

*And now abide faith, hope, love, these three; but the greatest of these is love (I Corinthians 13:13).*

*God is love (I John 4:8).*

Love is the foundation of scripture. Love is God's motive for sending Jesus to die. Love lasts forever and love is essential to the character and existence of God. How does that love come into our lives, fill our lives, and pour out of our lives? It happens because of the indwelling and abiding presence of the Holy Spirit in us. God fills us with love by the pouring of the Spirit into us. Love is manifest to us and through us because of the Spirit's fruitfulness of love inherent in His being. Love planted in us by the Holy Spirit who indwells us will grow, mature, and ripen. (It is the same for all flavors of the fruit of the Spirit).

John repeats the phrase, "God is love" later in chapter four when he writes:

*No one has seen God at any time. If we love one another, God abides in us, and his love has been perfected in us. By this we know that we abide in Him, and He in us, because he has given us of His Spirit…And we have known and believed the love that God has for us. God is love, and he who abides in love abides in God, and God in him (I John 4:12–13, 16).*

Loving one another is possible by the abiding Holy Spirit. Paul declares the same message: "Now hope does not disappoint, because the love of God has been poured out in our hearts by the holy Spirit who was given to us" (Romans 5:5). Love was poured into our hearts in the person of the Holy Spirit who is God and naturally emanates love.

Later, Paul begged the Christians in Rome "through the love of the Spirit" (Romans 15:30) to pray for him. Epaphras told Paul about the Colossians' "love in the Spirit" (Colossians 1:8). Love (like the other elements of the fruit of the Spirit) is the Spirit's, who wants you to have it by indwelling you, filling you, and producing His character and essential being in you.

You are the mission of the Holy Spirit! The Holy Spirit is on a mission and you are it! You are the mission field of God the Holy Spirit! He wants to "fruit" you with love, joy, peace, longsuffering, kindness, goodness, faithfulness, gentleness, and self-control.

Think on these things. Meditate.

# Mission 14: Gift You

Y ou are the mission of the Holy Spirit! The Holy Spirit is on a mission and you are it! You are the mission field of God the Holy Spirit! He wants to gift you.

God gives spiritual gifts to people when they become believers. Talents and personal abilities may be God-given when He creates individuals, but spiritual gifts are only given to Christians.

Chapters twelve, thirteen, and fourteen of I Corinthians are the most extensive and detailed teachings on spiritual gifts in the New Testament. (Romans 12 is a second major teaching on spiritual gifts). I Corinthians 12:4–11 specifically speaks of the Spirit's part in gifting individual believers:

> *Now there are diversities of gifts, but the same Spirit. There are differences of ministries, but the same Lord. And there are diversities of activities, but it is the same God who works all in all. But the manifestation of the Spirit is given to each one for the profit of all: for to one is given the word of wisdom through the Spirit, to another the word of knowledge through the same Spirit, to another faith by the same Spirit, to another gifts of healings by the same Spirit, to another the working of miracles, to another prophecy, to another discerning of spirits, to another different kinds of tongues, to another the interpretation of tongues. But one and the same Spirit works all these things, distributing to each one individually as He wills (I Corinthians 12:4–11).*

Simply, the Holy Spirit gives a variety of spiritual gifts to each believer as he wills, so other Christians will be edified and God will be glorified. Recognition and use of the gifts benefits the body of Christ—the church—so it is important to fellow believers that you know and share your spiritual gift(s). The following chart is what I use to help individual believers discover their gifts so they can use them to edify believers and honor God. This model is based on studying the original Greek New Testament word for spiritual gifts (*charismata*), and identifying the gifts given by the Spirit beginning at the Pentecost spoken of in Acts 2—the birth of the church.

## New Testament Spiritual Gifts

(Toward discerning, understanding, and using spiritual gifts)

Wisdom (I Corinthians 12:8)—Do I receive divine wisdom to share with others what comes from my communion with God? Do others seek my counsel regularly?

Knowledge (I Corinthians 12:8)—Do I receive information divinely revealed? Do messages come to me intellectually, academically, or situationally that could only have come from God?

Faith (I Corinthians 12:9)—Do I have a powerful faith that trusts and believes God for things that cannot be seen? Do I believe the answer or response is sure, even though there is no evidence that what I believe will come to pass?

Healings (I Corinthians 12:9)—Do people receive physical, emotional and spiritual healing when I pray for them? Are there immediate or accelerated healings when I pray for others?

Miracles (I Corinthians 12:10)—Do miraculous things happen from God when I am around and praying for divine intervention (i.e. divine provisions, exorcisms, divine protection, etc.)?

Prophecy (I Corinthians 12:10, Romans 12:6)—Does God enable me to foretell future events to His glory? Does God enable me to proclaim His message?

Discernment of Spirits (I Corinthians 12:10)—Do I discern good and evil easily? Can I detect if someone is lying or telling the truth? Do I perceive impure motives in others?

Tongues (I Corinthians 12:10)—Do I ever speak in a foreign language that I have never learned, but is native or learned of someone else and understood? Do I speak in a spiritual language that God has given me?

Interpretation of Tongues (I Corinthians 12:10)—Have I been able to understand a foreign language that I never learned? Have I interpreted a spiritual language that someone else spoke for the good of the body?

Helps (I Corinthians 12:28)—Am I a good helper? Would I rather assist someone else than be a leader? Do I tend to help others before I take care of my own needs? Do I get the job done by helping others do it?

Government/Administration (I Corinthians 12:28)—Am I able to organize and manage a group of workers and various activities and resources? Am I a coordinator-type person?

Ministry (Romans 12:7)—Do I love to serve others? Do I look for opportunities to minister to the needs of others? Do I look for ways to reach into others' lives and minister to them?

Teaching (Romans 12:7)—Do I have the ability to receive, understand, and share information and knowledge that has come to me from books and life? Are learners "my joy and my crown" as I see them receive my teachings?

Exhorting/Encouraging (Romans 12:8)—Do I share with others so that they are uplifted, not put down; encouraged, not discouraged; challenged, not condemned; built up, not torn down?

Giving (Romans 12:8)—Am I a "cheerful giver"? Do I enjoy giving myself and possessions to others? Am I generous?

Ruling/Leadership (Romans 12:8)—Am I a good example that others are willing to follow? Do I lead and guide others rather than administrate or dictate?

Mercy (Romans12:8)—Am I a compassionate and empathetic person? Do I want everything to be just right for everyone without hurts, heartaches, or friction? Do people in need touch my heart?


## NOTE:

Other scripture to be considered (not exhaustive) that are not specifically listed with or identified as spiritual gifts beginning at Pentecost:

Exodus 35:30–35 (tabernacle)—wisdom, understanding, knowledge, workmanship or craftsman (in gold, silver, brass, stone, wood, engraving, embroider, weaving)

Romans 12:13—hospitality (could be an expression of helps, giving, ministry, or mercy)

Colossians 1:9,10—intercessory prayer

Ephesians 5:18,19—music

---

At the end of I Corinthians 12, Paul wrote in verse 31 that he wanted to show the Corinthians something greater than gifts—love. I Corinthians 13 speaks of the supremacy of love, and then Paul returns to teachings about spiritual gifts in I Corinthians 14. Although Paul already taught that one gift is not more vital than the other, he writes about his preference of prophesying in Chapter 14.

As love is the primary slice/juice of the fruit of the Spirit, so prophecy is a primary spiritual gift by passion and preference, not preeminence and priority. It is one way that God the Holy Spirit wants to gift individuals. As we used love for an example of the Spirit "fruiting" you, so we use prophecy as an example of the Spirit gifting you.

Prophecy (*prophateia*) is commonly recognized as foretelling and forth telling.[10] It is a proclamation that the Holy Spirit gives you to declare future events or His specific message. In Mark 12:36, Jesus credits the Spirit as the source of David's prophetic words recorded in Psalm 110:1:

*For David himself said by the Holy Spirit: "The Lord said to my Lord, 'Sit at My right hand, till I make Your enemies Your footstool'" (Mark 12:36).*

God the Holy Spirit gave David a message he proclaimed, which was prophetically fulfilled in Jesus Christ.

Peter recognized the prophetic facet of David's ministry, too. In Acts 1, when the believers were looking for a replacement for Judas, Peter said:

*Men and brethren, this scripture had to be fulfilled, which the Holy Spirit spoke before by the mouth of David concerning Judas, who became a guide to those who arrested Jesus, "For he was numbered with us and obtained a part in this ministry. . . . For it is written in the book of Psalms [69:25, 109:8]: "Let his habitation be desolate, and let no one live in it;" and "Let another take his office" (Acts 1:16–17, 20).*

David, like all of the prophets of old, received messages from the Holy Spirit and proclaimed them knowing that God would fulfill them in the immediate or distant future.

Look at these two passages from Peter's writings:

*Of this salvation the prophets have inquired and searched diligently, who prophesied of the grace that would come to you, searching what, or what manner of time, the Spirit of Christ who was in them was indicating when He testified before hand the sufferings of Christ and the glories that would follow. To them it was revealed that, not to themselves, but to us they were ministering the things which now have been reported to you through those who have preached the gospel to you by the Holy Spirit sent from heaven--things which angels desire to look into (I Peter 1:10–12).*

*Knowing this first, that no prophecy of Scripture is of any private interpretation, for prophecy never came by the will of man, but holy men of God spoke as they were moved by the Holy Spirit (II Peter 1:20–21).*

The Old Testament prophets were temporarily indwelt by the Spirit of Christ— the Holy Spirit, and proclaimed their message. The Spirit left and returned with other prophesies.

In the New Covenant, God the Holy Spirit permanently indwells believers and gifts some of them with prophecy as He wills and is pleased. For example, when the prophet Agabus took Paul's belt and secured it around his own feet and hands, he prophesied:

*Thus says the Holy Spirit, so shall the Jews at Jerusalem bind the man who owns this belt, and deliver him into the hands of the Gentiles (Acts 21:11).*

The Jews sent Paul to Rome where he was imprisoned and later executed.

Now, back to the I Corinthians 14 passage, we see the gift of prophecy exemplifies the purpose and practice of all spiritual gifts. Verse one reminds us to "desire spiritual gifts." Verse three shows that these gifts, specifically prophecy, are to edify, exhort, and comfort. Prophesy is for the listener's benefit (I Corinthians 14:6). Verse nine teaches that prophecy is shared so that others can better understand the things of God. "Edification of the church" is highlighted in verse twelve. By extrapolation and application, I Corinthians 14:22–25 shows that spiritual gifts can be used to witness to unbelievers so they will acknowledge God.

Paul evidenced his own spiritual gifting of prophecy when he wrote:

> *Now the Spirit expressly says that in latter times some will depart from the faith, giving heed to deceiving spirits and doctrines of demons, speaking lies in hypocrisy, having their own conscience seared with a hot iron, forbidding to marry, and commanding to abstain from foods which God created to be received with thanksgiving by those who believe and know the truth (I Timothy 4:1–3).*

Paul said his source was the Holy Spirit. The Spirit delivered to Paul the message about the future. We read that message and understand its fulfillment in our day.

Since the Pentecost event (Acts 2), the Holy Spirit has gifted believers with spiritual gifts in the church to edify, encourage, comfort, co-labor, accomplish, unify, inform, witness, and ultimately, glorify God. He is the gift of God that gives gifts. May you realize the potential and possibilities of the Spirit's gift(s) in your life by having looked at the gift of prophecy.

You are the mission of the Holy Spirit! The Holy Spirit is on a mission and you are it! You are the mission field of God the Holy Spirit! He wants to gift you.

Think on these things. Meditate.

# Mission 15: Glorify Through You

Y ou are the mission of the Holy Spirit! The Holy Spirit is on a mission and you are it! You are the mission field of God the Holy Spirit! He wants to glorify God through you. He desires to glorify God the Father and God the Son through your life.

Jesus said of the Holy Spirit of truth, "He will glorify Me, for He will take of what is Mine and declare it to you" (John 16:14). This is a clear, direct, matter of fact statement that Jesus made about the ministry and mission of the Holy Spirit. The Spirit will take the teachings of Christ, all that pertains to Christ, and the ones who belong to Christ, and use them to glorify the Lord Jesus Christ. Paul wrote, "Therefore, whether you eat or drink, or whatever you do, do all to the glory of God" (I Corinthians 10:31). When the Holy Spirit takes control of your conscience, His mission will include God's glory through whatever you do in life—even through what you consume.

Our India mission team boarded the van at 10:00 p.m. preparing for the six-hour journey back to the city of Guntur. Our interpreter entered the vehicle and said, "They prepared supper for you." It was the Spirit's leading to go eat with them after our long journey to the village and our fierce spiritual warfare with the demon possessed. When some of the team hesitated and questioned partaking of the meal, the weeping interpreter said, "They have spent a week's wages on this meal. If you do not eat this meal, you will have undone all that God has done here today." We went to the dimly lit table. It was covered with woven leaf plates. They placed a *japoti* (like an oily tortilla) on our leaf plate. They put five different foods on our japoti with chicken being the only one that we recognized and identified. We prayed thanksgiving and sanctification over our food. Then we tore the japoti, wrapped the entrees inside, and placed them in our mouths. It was good. God was glorified because the Holy Spirit led us to eat that food.

Peter wrote:

> *If you are reproached for the name of Christ, blessed are you, for the Spirit of glory and of God rests upon you. On their part He is blasphemed, but on your part He is glorified (I Peter 4:14).*

Certainly, Jesus glorified His heavenly Father through His sufferings. Our suffering for Christ's sake brings glory to Him. As the Spirit of God and glory rests on you during reproach, Jesus is glorified. God the Holy Spirit desires to glorify God the Son, and through our trials and reproaches the Spirit makes possible the glorification of Jesus Christ. When Jesus' glory is revealed, we will rejoice that the Spirit led us through the suffering to manifest the glory of the Lord Jesus.

II Corinthians 3: 7–18 is a powerful passage that speaks about the continued work of the Spirit and the increasing glory that happens through our lives. Paul is doing a comparative between the old and new covenants, the letter and the Spirit, and the past and present manifestations of the glory of God. The old expression of God's manifested glory is called a ministry of death, condemnation, external, fading, Mosaic, and less than the glory now revealed. The new manifestation of His glory is called the ministry of the Spirit—righteousness—that which excels, remains, liberates, transforms, and increases. It is the mission of the Holy Spirit to transform us into the image of Christ with ever-increasing glory.

> *But we all, with unveiled face, beholding as in a mirror the glory of the Lord, are being transformed into the same image from glory to glory, just as by the Spirit of the Lord (II Corinthians 3:18).*

You are the mission of the Holy Spirit! The Holy Spirit is on a mission and you are it! You are the mission field of God the Holy Spirit! He wants to glorify Jesus and the Father through you with increasing glory.

Think on these things. Meditate.

# Mission 16: Guide You

Y ou are the mission of the Holy Spirit! The Holy Spirit is on a mission and you are it! You are the mission field of God the Holy Spirit! He wants to divinely lead and guide you.

"What is the leading of the Holy Spirit in this matter?" This question is the ultimate question that we try to answer when we are seeking God's guidance in any matter. We look for clear leadings of the Holy Spirit in every matter no matter what the matter is that we are facing at the moment.

A variety of English concepts are used to communicate this facet of the Spirit's mission in our lives. The Lordship of the Holy Spirit (II Corinthians 3:17) inherently includes this dynamic of our "followship." He is Lord and guides us as part of that Lordship. Sometimes the Bible teaches us that the Spirit prompts, provokes, purposes, leads, drives, constrains, compels, controls, influences, and presses us. Other times, the Spirit directs our path by forbidding or restraining us from going to certain places or doing certain things.

It is always exciting for me to see a teaching exemplified in the life of Jesus, experienced in the New Testament Church, and explained in other biblical teachings. The guidance of God the Holy Spirit is one of those topics. The leading of the Holy Spirit in the life of Jesus is exemplified in events like the temptation of Christ. The three Synoptic Gospels (Matthew, Mark, and Luke) all record this story. Matthew used the word "led" (Greek—*anachtha*) saying that "Jesus was led up by the Spirit into the wilderness to be tempted by the devil" (Matthew 4:1).[11] Mark recorded the event by writing "the Spirit drove Him into the wilderness" as he used the Greek word *ekballei* (Mark 1:12).[12] Luke used the Greek concept *ageto* commonly translated "led" (Luke 4:1).[13] Jesus was led, guided, compelled, or driven by the Holy Spirit into the wilderness. Luke added that Jesus was "filled" with the Spirit and then "led" by the Spirit. The filling of the Spirit preceded the leading of the Spirit. Obedience and fellowship more likely transpire when we are Spirit-filled.

The leading and guidance of the Holy Spirit has a fascinating twist in John 3:8. After Jesus told Nicodemus that he had to be born again, He said:

> *The wind blows where it wishes and you hear the sound of it, but cannot tell where it comes from and where it goes. So is everyone who is born of the Spirit. (John 3:8).*

The Holy Spirit blows, leads, guides, and propels believers where He wills at the rate, time, distance, and destination that He desires. Sometimes the leadings don't make sense to us. The direction or action is irrational at times like the oddities of our western Kansas wind storms. The wind can do some wild, strange, and unbelievable things because of its enormous power and uncontained properties. We have seen wheat straw driven into fence posts. Snow drifts were blown as high as the house. Darkness occurred at midday because the wind filled the sky with dust. Born-again believers should be windblown. The Spirit is the Wind that blows us.

The Christian commands from God are usually the opposite of the world's directives. Not all of God's leadings and personal commands in the Bible have been rational, reasonable, or in decent order from the human perspective. The prophets were given some wild things to say and do. Moses, Abraham, and others were given some directives that didn't make sense at the time. Of course, the greatest example of the wind blowing the opposite of our expected direction is the incarnation, crucifixion, and resurrection of Jesus Christ.

The Holy Spirit will lead in truth, even if His Guidance doesn't make sense to us. Jesus promised, "However, when He, the Spirit of truth, has come, He will Guide you into all truth" (John 16:13a). First of all, note that the Holy Spirit is the Spirit of truth. Truth is essential to His being since He is God. Second, His guidance is in all truth. He will lead you in the truth of the scriptures. The Spirit will not violate the Word that He inspired. His directions for your life will be consistent with His character and existence.

It is also fascinating to see the wind blow through the New Testament Church. Some of the Holy Spirit's specific directions made sense to the recipients of His divine guidance, and at other times people couldn't understand His plan. Look at some of these examples in the early church after the rushing mighty wind of the Spirit at Pentecost. See the Spirit lead Philip as recorded in Acts 8. An angel told Philip to leave the high action of Jerusalem to go to the deserted place of Gaza. Here he encountered the Ethiopian eunuch whom God was going to use to take the Gospel to Candace, the queen of Ethiopia. Philip had to run and catch the chariot of the eunuch, make sense out of the Isaiah passage the Eunuch was reading, and then baptize the new believer. Why? Because the Spirit said to Philip, "Go near and overtake this chariot" (Acts 8:29).

The Spirit told Peter about three men seeking him and directed him to go with them without doubt (Acts 10:19 and 11:12). Peter could not make sense out of the leading until the Holy Spirit was poured out on the Gentiles at Cornelius' place just like the blowing wind on the Jews in Jerusalem at Pentecost.

Missions were birthed because the Holy Spirit sent out Saul (Paul) and Barnabas to do a new work that had not been performed in the past. Luke recorded:

> *As they ministered to the Lord and fasted, the Holy Spirit said, "Now separate to me Barnabas and Saul for the work to which I have called them. Then having fasted and prayed, and laid hands on them, they sent them away. So, being sent out by the Holy Spirit, they went down to Seleucia, and from there they sailed to Cyprus. (Acts 13:2–4).*

The Spirit sent them originally and continued to guide them. The divine guidance of the Holy Spirit took on different forms and patterns along the way. He acted like the wind. It is recorded in Acts 16:6 that the missionaries "were forbidden by the Holy Spirit to preach the word in Asia." Did God forbid preaching in Asia at that time because He didn't want the Asians to hear the gospel and be saved? Absolutely not! But the Spirit was flowing as He willed to spread the gospel to the places and people He desired on His time frame and according to His plan. In Acts 16:7 we read, ". . . they tried to go into Bithynia, but the Spirit did not permit them." Why? The leading of the Holy Spirit for that time was to get them to go to Macedonia.

In Act 18:5 we see that Paul was "constrained by the Spirit and testified to the Jews that Jesus is the Christ." The Holy Spirit compelled Paul to share the gospel of Christ. Acts 19:21 tells us that Paul "purposed in the Spirit" to go to Jerusalem and Rome. The Holy Spirit impressed a desire into Paul's heart to go to these two cities and give testimony to Jesus Christ. This purpose was not thwarted when some disciples told Paul not to go to Jerusalem as the Spirit told them (Acts 21:4). Paul and the disciples all knew that opposition and persecution awaited him in Jerusalem because of the message of the Spirit. The disciples did not want Paul to face what the Spirit revealed, but he was determined to follow the leading of the Holy Spirit no matter the cost.

Romans 8:14 says, "For as many as are led by the Spirit of God, these are the sons of God." This powerful teaching reminds us that one of the evidences of being a born-again child of God is a Spirit-led life. We are not driven by the external law. We are led by the Spirit (Galatians 5:18). We go with the flow of the wind. We live a yielded life. We put up our sails of surrender and let the wind blow us as He wills. We used to take the corners of our windbreakers and pull them up behind our backs at recess. The western Kansas winds would blow against the windbreaker and cause us to run faster than we could on our own power.

You are the mission of the Holy Spirit. The Holy Spirit is on a mission and you are it. You are the mission field of God the Holy Spirit. He wants to lead and guide you.

Think on these things. Meditate.

# Mission 17: Heart You

Y ou are the mission of the Holy Spirit! The Holy Spirit is on a mission and you are it! You are the mission field of God the Holy Spirit! He wants to "heart" you.

First, God has always been a God of the heart. He desires truth, relationship, and life to be a matter of the heart. When Samuel went to locate a successor to king Saul, he approached God's task with an earthly perspective. God's criteria was an internal, spiritual, character qualification rather than an external, appearance, physical measure. Samuel thought that he had met God's anointed future king when he saw Eliab. But God said to the prophet Samuel:

*Do not look at his appearance or at the height of his stature, because I have refused him. For the Lord does not see as man sees, for man looks at the outward appearance, but the Lord looks at the heart (I Samuel 16:7).*

God looks at the inner person, the character, the deepest part of an individual being where motives and integrity are birthed and holiness and purity reside. Christ-likeness and godly perspective are the foundations of the heart that the Spirit wants to breathe into us.

Second, the heart matter is an essential element of our salvation. Paul wrote to the Romans:

*...that if you confess with your mouth the Lord Jesus and believe in your heart that God has raised Him from the dead, you will be saved. For with the heart one believes to righteousness, and with the mouth confession is made to salvation (Romans 10:9,10).*

The heart is the spiritual functional part of the soul that is responsive to God at salvation. It is the place of divine perspective, character, and the deepest point of spiritual response to God.

The Spirit and flesh distinction shed some light on how the Spirit wants to "heart" you. Romans 1:4 reminds us that the Christ, who was born of the fleshly descent of David, was "declared to be the Son of God with power, according to the Spirit of holiness, by the resurrection from the dead." An earthly familial lineage was externally traceable and recorded. The internal character and person were identified by the Holy Spirit of power evidenced by the resurrection.

In the Romans 2:25–29 teaching on circumcision and uncircumcision, Paul points out the difference between the physical and spiritual acts with this astounding teaching:

*For he is not a Jew who is one outwardly, nor is that circumcision which is outward in the flesh; but he is a Jew who is one inwardly, and circumcision is that of the heart, in the Spirit, and not in the letter; whose praise is not from men but from God (Romans 2:28–29).*

It is the Spirit that makes a matter a heart issue and not a mere flesh issue. There is a definite distinction in living by the spiritual heart and not according to the flesh. Paul wrote:

*For the flesh lusts against the Spirit, and the Spirit against the flesh; and these are contrary to one another, so that you do not do the things that you wish (Galatians 5:17).*

There is a major contrast between the heart and the flesh. The Holy Spirit is the difference maker. You can go through the motions and do the externals for a time, but the internal heart dynamics are a matter of the Spirit. The Spirit wants you to be cardiac compelled.

You are the mission of the Holy Spirit! The Holy Spirit is on a mission and you are it! You are the mission field of God the Holy Spirit! He wants to "heart" you with the internal, spiritual, character motivation, and perspective of Jesus Christ.

Think on these things. Meditate.

# Mission 18: Hope You

Y ou are the mission of the Holy Spirit! The Holy Spirit is on a mission and you are it! You are the mission field of God the Holy Spirit. He wants to "hope" you.

Olu Menjay, the head of Ricks Institute in Liberia always says, "Come hope us." He doesn't say the usual, "Come help us." He wants us to come stir up hope for them. Olu knows that the fourteen years of civil war in his country, among other devastations, destroyed hope. Olu believes in the ministry of hope, and we cannot have genuine hope apart from God—Father, Son, and Holy Spirit.

Romans 5:1–5 is one of my all-time favorite passages. In these verses, we read these powerful encouraging words: "Now hope does not disappoint, because the love of God has been poured out in our hearts by the Holy Spirit who was given to us" (Romans 5:5). We are not disappointed when it comes to hope in God because we are indwelt. The Holy Spirit continuously reminds us that we have hope for all eternity. We will not be disappointed when we enter heaven. Eternity with God in heaven will not fall short of our expectations. Until we get to heaven, the indwelling Holy Spirit gives us hope by His presence in us.

The Spirit's mission not only makes hope a reality by His indwelling, but He also makes hope abundant by His power.

> *Now may the God of hope fill you with all joy and peace in believing,     that you may abound in hope by the power of the Holy Spirit (Romans 15:13).*

God (Father, Son, and Holy Spirit) is all about present and increasing hope. God is the source of all hope, period. The Spirit who glorifies Jesus reminds us of the simple message that God the Son is, ". . .the Lord Jesus Christ, our hope" (I Timothy 1:1b). The Spirit wants to "hope" us by His indwelling presence and by the growing realities of hope in our lives. He wants hope to invade every facet of our lives. The Spirit desires hope to permeate all dimensions of life. He craves a growing, abounding, increased hope in our lives.

Hope has present and future dynamics. There are present realities and future possibilities of hope. Paul wrote to the Galatians, "For we through the Spirit eagerly wait for the hope of righteousness by faith" (Galatians 5:5). On the one hand, we presently have his righteousness by faith. On the other hand, we are obtaining His righteousness by faith. Our future hope is to receive His righteousness in its fullness. Spiritual maturing and growth give us the reality of this present and future hope.

You are the mission of the Holy Spirit! The Holy Spirit is on a mission and you are it! You are the mission field of God the Holy Spirit! He wants to "hope" you.

Think on these things. Meditate.

# Mission 19: Inspire You

Y ou are the mission of the Holy Spirit! The Holy Spirit is on a mission and you are it! You are the mission field of God the Holy Spirit! He wants to inspire you.

A basic tenet of the Christian faith is that the Holy Spirit inspired the writing of God's Word (II Timothy 3:16). Literally, the scriptures were God-breathed.[14] The Holy Spirit inspired the prophetic word that came from God by breathing it into men for all human kind. God the Holy Spirit wants you to live a Spirit-breathed inspired life.

Our very expressions and acts of worship are to be Spirit-inspired because, "God is Spirit, and those who worship Him must worship Him in spirit and truth" (John 4:24). The Ultimate Spirit Being is in us as Christians and prompts us, compels us, motivates us, and inspires us to declare His worth. We are moved to pray and sing by the Spirit.

> *What is the result then? I will pray with the spirit, and I will also pray with understanding, I will sing with the spirit, and I will also sing with understanding. (I Corinthians 14:15).*

Part of being Spirit-filled is, "speaking to one another in psalms and hymns and spiritual songs, singing, and making melody in your heart to the Lord" (Ephesians 5:19). Part of the functional aspects of having the full armor of God is, "praying always with all prayers and supplications in the Spirit" (Ephesians 6:18). Paul wrote, "For we are the circumcision, who worship God in the Spirit, rejoice in Christ Jesus, and have no confidence in the flesh" (Philippians 3:3). The Holy Spirit inspires worship through singing and prayer.

The Spirit-breathed life is not only inspired worship, prayer, and singing, but it is the continuous growth and edification of a maturing faith. Jude said it this way:

> *But you, beloved, building yourselves up on your most holy faith, praying in the Holy Spirit, keep yourselves in the love of God, looking for the mercy of our Lord Jesus Christ unto eternal life (Jude 1:20–21).*

Every building block of your personal faith is inspired by the Spirit. Every fiber and expression of God's sustaining love in your life is Spirit-breathed. Every anticipation and hope for eternity is Spirit-inspired. Every leading, inspiration, prayer, song, prophesy, directive, motivation, and ministry that happens in your life is God-breathed.

You are the mission of the Holy Spirit! The Holy Spirit is on a mission and you are it! You are the mission field of God the Holy Spirit! He wants to inspire you.

Think on these things. Meditate.

# Mission 20: Intercede for You

Y ou are the mission of the Holy Spirit! The Holy Spirit is on a mission and you are it! You are the mission field of God the Holy Spirit! He wants to intercede for you.

Romans 8:26–27 are the verses that inspired the song "Holy Spirit Intercede." The God-breathed words of these two verses are:

> *Likewise the Spirit also helps in our weaknesses. For we do not know what we should pray for as we ought, but the Spirit Himself makes intercession for us with groanings which cannot be uttered. Now He who searches the hearts knows what the mind of the Spirit is, because He makes intercession for the saints according to the will of God (Romans 8:26–27).*

The intercessory prayer ministry of the Holy Spirit is multifaceted. He is the Helper that aids us in prayer because we do not know what to say to God the Father. We are weak and frail when it comes to praying as we should according to God's will. The Spirit not only helps us with the right words, but He Himself intercedes for us when there are no human words to speak the deep things of God. The human voice cannot even make the sounds that the Spirit uses to intercede for us. He not only helps us to pray, but when we are beyond help and human capacity to pray, He gets our needed requests to the Father via exclusive Spirit prayer. The Lord Jesus, who is the Spirit, (II Corinthians 3:17), "ever lives to make intercession" for us (Hebrews 7:25). We can be assured that our humanly unspeakable requests get to God the Father by the Holy Spirit.

Take the challenge to meditate on the lyrics of the song, "Holy Spirit Intercede." When you have finished rehearsing the words, spend some time in absolute silence. Be still, and continue contemplating the intercessory prayer mission of the Holy Spirit. Focus on the reality that God the Holy Spirit is praying for you in the moment. He is interceding for you right now!

## HOLY SPIRIT INTERCEDE

Only Your Spirit can pray
Whatever we cannot say.
Holy Spirit, intercede.

When we can't find the word,
May it in heaven be heard.
Holy Spirit, intercede.

We are frail;
Help us in our weakness.

We don't know what to pray;
Please groan what we can't speak
Holy Spirit, intercede.

Only Your Spirit can pray
Whatever we cannot say.
Holy Spirit, intercede.

When we can't find the word,
May it in heaven be heard.
Holy Spirit, intercede.

We are frail;
Help us in our weakness.
We don't know what to pray;
Please pray the Father's will.
Holy Spirit, intercede.

Only Your Spirit can pray
Whatever we cannot say.
Holy Spirit, intercede.

When we can't find the word,
May it in heaven be heard.
Holy Spirit, intercede.

You are the mission of the Holy Spirit! The Holy Spirit is on a mission and you are it! You are the mission field of God the Holy Spirit! He wants to intercede for you. He is interceding for you right now!

Think on these things. Meditate.

# Mission 21: Justify You

Y ou are the mission of the Holy Spirit! The Holy Spirit is on a mission and you are it! You are the mission field of God the Holy Spirit! He wants to justify you.

We were taught in Sunday School that the big word "justified" meant "just as if I'd never sinned." The rebirthing salvation of the Spirit makes us right with God. There is no record of our wrong. We are declared just before a Holy God. This is a work of God the Holy Spirit. The apostle Paul wrote:

> *And such were some of you. But you were washed, but you were sanctified, but you were justified in the name of the Lord Jesus and by the Spirit of our God (I Corinthians 6:11).*

Justification happened in the name (the person, power, and character) of Jesus Christ the Lord and by God's Spirit. The Holy Spirit washes our sin and ungodly lifestyle away from us. He sanctifies, sets us apart, makes us holy, and causes us to be delivered from the transgressions and impurities of our sins. From the list in I Corinthians 6:9–10 we could say that fornicators no longer fornicate and are considered by God to have never committed fornication in their lives. Idolaters cease their idol worship and are considered by God to have never committed idolatry. Adulterers stop committing adultery and are treated by God as if they had never committed adultery. Homosexuals and sodomites no longer commit homosexual acts or sodomy and are considered by God to have never performed homosexual acts or sodomy. Thieves stop stealing and have no record of having ever stolen any goods. The covetous ones stop lusting after the possessions of others and are considered by God to have never coveted before in their whole lives. It is like the teaching of II Corinthians 5:17: "If anyone is in Christ, he is a new creation; old things have passed away; behold, all things have become new." This is the justifying mission of the Holy Spirit.

I Timothy 3:16 is a beautiful summation of the life of Jesus, God in the flesh, with a little twist to the justifying ministry of the Holy Spirit.

> *And without controversy great is the mystery of godliness: God was manifested in the flesh, justified in the Spirit, seen by angels preached among the Gentiles, believed on in the world, received up in glory (I Timothy 3:16).*

God became a man—Jesus Christ of Nazareth. He never sinned and therefore never needed to be justified because of his personal sin. Jesus—God in human existence—was justified by the Spirit for the sins of others: "For He made Him who knew no sin to be sin for us, that we might become the righteousness of God in Him" (II Corinthians 5:21). The Spirit verified and validated that Jesus was the Just One. He confirmed Jesus at His baptism when He descended on Jesus like a dove. The Spirit justified Jesus when He died for the sins of the world and took the place of sinners on the cross, being treated as their sin. He justified Jesus when He raised Him from the dead "and declared [Him] to be the Son of God with power, according to the Spirit of holiness, by the resurrection from the dead . . ."(Romans 1:4).

You are the mission of the Holy Spirit! The Holy Spirit is on a mission and you are it! You are the mission field of God the Holy Spirit! He wants to justify you. He wants you to be right with God and stop the sinful lifestyle that you live. He wants you to be just as if you had never sinned.

Think on these things. Meditate.

# Mission 22: Manifest and Reveal to You

Y ou are the mission of the Holy Spirit! The Holy Spirit is on a mission and you are it! You are the mission field of God the Holy Spirit! He wants to manifest and reveal Himself in and through your life.

My graduate course entitled "Death and Dying" included a session with spiritualists for some strange reason. They were trying to connect with the class by saying things like, "I perceive that someone in this area was in a motorcycle wreck." They kept guessing wrong. I turned to the guy next to me who was wearing a neck brace. I said to this total stranger, "I perceive that there is something wrong with your neck." He laughed and replied, "Yes! I'm falling apart!" He proceeded to tell me about his degenerative bone disease that was eroding his neck bones and making its way down his spine. God the Holy Spirit wants to manifest Himself clearly so it is not a guessing game nor a self-reliant source.

Scriptures that come to mind as I think of the manifesting and revealing mission of the Holy Spirit are quite varied. The Joel 2:28–29 prophecy that Peter quoted at Pentecost (Acts 2:16–18) included an outpouring of the Spirit, God-given prophecies, dreams, and visions. All of these are forms of revealings and manifestations. The Spirit is on a mission to pour Himself out on us and to give us prophesies, dreams, and visions. He initiates all of these manifestations, so that they are part of His missionary work in us. This is a generic record of the manifest ministry of the Spirit, but there are specific examples of His revealing mission, too.

Simeon, who held Jesus when He was eight days old at His baby dedication, was a mission field of the Holy Spirit. It is said of Simeon,

> *... the Holy Spirit was upon him. And it had been revealed to him by the Holy Spirit that he would not see death before he had seen the Lord's Christ. So he came by the Spirit into the temple. And when the parents brought in the Child Jesus, to do for Him according to the custom of the law, he took Him up in his arms and blessed God and said ... (Luke 2:25–28).*

The Spirit revealed a particular encounter that Simeon would experience before his death. The Spirit led him to a specific place at the perfect time to manifest Himself and that promise. The revealing of the Spirit was manifested precisely as He determined.

Other specific New Testament examples of the Holy Spirit's detailed manifestations and revealings include individuals like the prophet Agabus. The Spirit showed him "that there was going to be a great famine throughout all of the world ..." (Acts 11:28). At Tyre, disciples, "told Paul through the Spirit not to go to Jerusalem" (Acts 21:4). Paul knew that the signs and miracles that were part of his proclamation of the Gospel were manifestations "by the power of the Spirit of God" (Romans 15:19).

Look at Paul's teaching that the Holy Spirit gave him as recorded in I Corinthians 2:10–12 after quoting Isaiah 64:4:

> *But God has revealed them to us through His Spirit. For the Spirit searches all things, yes, the deep things of God. For what man knows the things of a man except the Spirit of the man which is in him? Even so no one knows the things of God except the Spirit of God. Now we have received, not the spirit of the world, but the Spirit who is from God, that we might know the things that have been freely given to us by God (I Corinthians 2:10–12).*

The Spirit has now revealed what previously had not been seen, nor heard, nor manifest in man's heart about God's dynamics of love for us. Since we have been given the Holy Spirit who knows God's thoughts, we can receive the unveiling of God's thoughts. Paul concludes that "we have the mind of Christ" (I Corinthians 2:16) in the giving of the Spirit who is a Revealer.

I Corinthians 12:7 reminds us that the spiritual gifts are individual manifestations of the Spirit for all to use to benefit the whole body. Paul identified the Corinthian believers as a manifest letter of Christ written "by the Spirit of the living God" (II Corinthians 3:3). The apostle also recorded that the message to him concerning the Gentiles being joint heirs with Jewish believers was a "revelation" of the Spirit (Ephesians 3:3–6). Paul echoed that message in Galatians 3:14:

> *. . . that the blessing of Abraham might come upon the Gentiles in Christ Jesus, that we might receive the promise of the Spirit through faith (Galatians 3:14).*

The writer of Hebrews wrote of the Holy of Holies:

> *. . . the Holy Spirit indicating this, that the way into the Holiest of all was not yet made manifest while the first tabernacle was still standing (Hebrews 9:8).*

The Spirit revealed then and wants to declare to us now that the complete sacrifice made in the Holy of Holies was only made by the Priest Jesus. Jesus is the only way into the now accessible Holiest place by the Spirit because the curtain was torn in two.

And, of course, we could not leave the manifesting and revealing mission of the Holy Spirit without some reflection on The Book of the Revelation. The Spirit that inspired the scriptures and whose purpose is to glorify Jesus breathed these words into the apostle John. "The Revelation of Jesus Christ . . ."(Revelation 1:1). The revealings of God are about His Son and manifested by the Holy Spirit to be heard and obeyed. "I was in the Spirit on the Lord's Day . . ."(Revelation 1:10). Seven times in the Book of the Revelation we are told "He who has an ear, let him hear what the Spirit says to the churches" (Rev. 2:7, 11,17, 29, 3:6, 13, 22). Chapter 4 begins with the trumpet of the Lord as in 1:10, but rather than commanding John to see, write, and send, He invites him to "Come up here, and I will show you things which must take place after this"

(Revelation 4:1b). God wanted John to join Him to reveal future events to him. John would have the indescribable privilege to see the unveilings from God's view. Wow!

The very next thing we read in the Bible after this phenomenal invitation is, "Immediately, I was in the Spirit; and behold, a throne set in heaven, and One sat on the throne" (Revelation 4:2). He was "in the Spirit" as in Revelation 1:10, and the revealings began to unfold once again. The phrase "in the Spirit" is used two more times in the Book of the Revelation where John is carried away to see other manifestations in the wilderness (Revelation 17:3) and on a high mountain to view the holy New Jerusalem (Revelation 21:10). "Worship God! For the testimony of Jesus is the spirit of prophesy" (Revelation 19:10).

You are the mission of the Holy Spirit! The Holy Spirit is on a mission and you are it! You are the mission field of God the Holy Spirit! He wants to manifest and reveal Himself to you in every facet of life. He wants to declare Himself and point you to Jesus through scriptures, dreams, visions, prophecies, divine invitations, outpourings, sovereign interventions, clear leadings, specific instructions, particular encounters, new things not formerly revealed, the thoughts of Christ's mind, spiritual gifts, access to the Holy of Holies, and the entire thrust and dynamics of the Book of the Revelation and spirit of prophecy.

Think on these things. Meditate.

# Mission 23: Minister Through You

Y ou are the mission of the Holy Spirit! The Holy Spirit is on a mission and you are it! You are the mission field of God the Holy Spirit! He wants to minister through you.

It amazes me that the same night I began to write this chapter is the very evening our international cell group started with the identical verse.

> *But now we have been delivered from the law, having died to what we were held by, so that we should serve in the newness of the Spirit and not in the oldness of the letter (Romans 7:6).*

Service or ministry, (one of the spiritual gifts) is done in the Spirit. The Holy Spirit who lives in us wants to reach out of us and touch other lives. He wants to care for others through you. He wants to supply the needs of others through you. He wants to minister the Word of God to others through you. All ministries happen in the power, motivation, conviction, and love of the Holy Spirit. It is like Jesus saying, "I am the vine, you are the branches. He who abides in Me, and I in him, bears much fruit; for without Me you can do nothing" (John 15:5).

Paul contrasts the New Covenant ministry of the Spirit with the Old Covenant letter of the law which shows how the Holy Spirit ministers to and through believers.

> *Not that we are sufficient of ourselves to think of anything as being from ourselves, but our sufficiency is from God, who also made us sufficient as ministers of the new covenant, not of the letter but of the Spirit; for the letter kills, but the Spirit gives life. But if the ministry of death, written and engraved on stones, was glorious, so that the children of Israel could not look steadily at the face of Moses because of the glory of his countenance, which glory was passing away, how will the ministry of the Spirit not be more glorious? For if the ministry of condemnation had glory, the ministry of righteousness exceeds much more in glory. For even what was made glorious had no glory in this respect, because of the glory that excels. For if what is passing away was glorious, what remains is much more glorious ( II Corinthians 3:5–11).*

This passage clearly shows that New Covenant ministry happens because of the sufficiency of God and the life-giving dynamic of the Holy Spirit. These verses reflect on how the glorious ministry of God the Holy Spirit exceeds the glorious ministry of Moses and the Ten Commandments received directly from God on the mountain. The Old Covenant ministry is identified in this text as "the ministry of death, engraved on stones . . . glorious . . . passing away . . . the ministry of condemnation." The New Covenant ministry of the Spirit is recognized as "more glorious . . . the ministry of righteousness . . . glory that excels." God the Holy Spirit's ministry to us and through us promotes His righteousness and excessive glory. It is what He does in and through our lives, "for it is God who works in you both to will and to do for His good pleasure" (Philippians 2:13).

You are the mission of the Holy Spirit! The Holy Spirit is on a mission and you are it! You are the mission field of God the Holy Spirit! Be yielded and surrendered to Him because He wants to minister things of the Spirit to you and through you.

Think on these things. Meditate.

# Mission 24: Prosper You

You are the mission of the Holy Spirit! The Holy Spirit is on a mission and you are it! You are the mission field of God the Holy Spirit! He wants to prosper you.

If financial prosperity and earthly riches are the evidences of spiritual maturity and success, then Jesus was an immature pauper who spiritually failed. If earthly wealth is a sign of spiritual maturity, then there are a ton of impoverished Christian martyrs who are suffering as spiritual babes in Christ. God is the source of wealth. The scriptures show righteous and wicked people prospering financially in diverse situations. God's impartation of earthly riches is ultimately for the fulfillment of His purposes.

God the Holy Spirit is concerned about the dynamics of spiritual prosperity. Proverbs 28:13 is an example of spiritual prosperity and spiritual concerns: "He who covers his sins will not prosper, But whoever confesses and forsakes them will have mercy." Confessed and forsaken sins lead to forgiveness and mercy, not necessarily wealth and money.

The sowing and reaping principle of scripture is also relevant to this discussion:

> Do not be deceived, God is not mocked; for whatever a man sows that he will also reap. For he who sows to his flesh will of the flesh reap corruption, but he who sows to the Spirit will of the Spirit reap everlasting life. And let us not grow weary while doing good, for in due season we shall reap if we do not lose heart (Galatians 6:7–9).

Sowing to the Spirit reaps a harvest of spiritual things.

The lyrics of Psalm 118:25–26 were echoed at the triumphal entry of Jesus into Jerusalem: "Save now, I pray, O Lord . . . blessed is he who comes in the name of the Lord . . ." A phrase not quoted but inserted between the familiar proclamations of Palm Sunday is, "O Lord, I pray, send now prosperity" (Psalm 118:25). A people who wanted deliverance from Roman oppression and were craving the Messiah's rule were not focused on finances. They wanted the kingdom of God to reign on earth and they expected to enjoy the peace and benefits of His government.

Jesus taught what was profitable and the source of genuine prosperity. He gave this instruction to His followers: "It is the Spirit who gives life, the flesh profits nothing. The words that I speak to you are spirit and they are life" (John 6:63). Jesus' teachings aimed at the spirit to affect lives. The Holy Spirit brings to us the prosperity of new life from Jesus' teachings. Jesus raised the question, "For what will it profit a man if he gains the whole world, and loses his own soul?" (Mark 8:36). To the rich, young ruler he said, "If you want to be perfect, go, sell what you have and give to the poor, and you will have treasure in heaven; and come, follow Me" (Matthew 19:21). Jesus' parable of the rich man who planned to tear down his barns and build bigger barns concluded:

*But God said to him, "You fool! This night your soul will be required of you; then whose will those things be which you have provided?" So is he who lays up treasure for himself, and is not rich toward God (Luke 12:20–21).*

Numerous other teachings reflect on earthly wealth and the spiritual prosperity that the Holy Spirit wants to provide for us. Paul wrote to the Philippians:

*For I know that this will turn out for my salvation through your prayer and the supply of the Spirit of Jesus Christ,. . . for to me, to live is Christ and to die is gain (Philippians 1:19, 21).*

God supplies His Spirit for spiritual prosperity and gain. The Holy Spirit is the source and resource of your spiritual prosperity. Jesus said:

*If you then, being evil, know how to give good gifts to your children, how much more will your heavenly Father give the Holy Spirit to those who ask Him! (Luke 11:13).*

More Holy Spirit produces more spiritual prosperity in our lives. The reason Jesus was the most prosperous individual in the whole world for all times, in the context of spiritual prosperity is found in John 3:34: "For He whom God has sent speaks the words of God, for God does not give the Spirit by measure." Jesus, truly God and truly man, was given the Holy Spirit without limit.

You are the mission of the Holy Spirit! The Holy Spirit is on a mission and you are it! You are the mission field of God the Holy Spirit! He wants to prosper you with spiritual prosperity.

Think on these things. Meditate.

# Mission 25: Rebirth You

You are the mission of the Holy Spirit! The Holy Spirit is on a mission and you are it! You are the mission field of God the Holy Spirit! He wants to rebirth you, adopt you, regenerate you.

When the Pharisee Nicodemus secretly came to Jesus at night and observed that His teachings and miracles were from God, Jesus answered: "Most assuredly, I say to you, unless one is born again, he cannot see the kingdom Of God" (John 3:3). If a person is not born again, he cannot see God's kingdom. You will not see earthly glimpses of the kingdom nor the eternal fullness of God's kingdom. Even the visible and observable facets of the kingdom will be invisible to you. Furthermore, in Jesus and Nicodemus' dialogue, the Pharisee inquired how an individual could physically be born again. Jesus replied:

> Most assuredly, I say to you, unless one is born of water and the Spirit, he cannot enter the kingdom of God. That which is born of the flesh is flesh, and that which is born of the Spirit is spirit. Do not marvel that I said to you, "You must be born again" (John 3:5–7).

Unless you are born again by the Spirit, you will not see nor enter the kingdom of God. Nicodemus, like us many times, tried to comprehend the things of the Spirit with the rational of the flesh. We try to find reasonable solutions or interpretations to the teachings and leadings of God the Holy Spirit. Nicodemus' mother was potentially deceased. If his mother was dead, she would have to be resurrected, he would have to shrink down in size, and re-enter her womb. She would have to go through birth pangs and delivery so he could be birthed a second time. Water would come rushing out of her at the birth of her son, Nicodemus, just like the first time he was born. This would not be a new spiritual birth, but a recycled physical birth. It would be like some novel form of reincarnation or human cloning of ourselves. It would be irrational thinking of our God-given brain to use common sense to understand spiritual rebirth. God the Holy Spirit wants you be born again with His rebirthing process. His mission for you is not another physical water birth, but a spiritual Spirit rebirth. His desire for you is a new heavenly birth where you can see and enter God's kingdom. The rebirth is for a functional purpose in addition to entering and seeing God's kingdom. The last part of Jesus' answer to Nicodemus' second question helps to reveal that purpose. Jesus continued:

> The wind blows where it wishes, and you hear the sound of it, but cannot tell where it comes from and where it goes. So is everyone who is born of the Spirit (John 3:8).

The purpose of being born again is not only our personal benefits of seeing and entering the kingdom, but also to know the invisible presence of the Holy Spirit and go where He blows/leads you to the glorification of Jesus Christ. Be yielded and surrendered to the Holy Spirit to rebirth you into God's kingdom and guide you in living in His kingdom as His children. Other concepts that highlight being born again are adoption and regeneration. Adoption, in the natural sense of the term, refers to receiving a child born to someone else into your family as your own offspring. Spiritual adoption happens when a person receives the Holy Spirit into his spirit and He (the Spirit) rebirths them into God's family as His own offspring. Paul wrote it like this:

> For you did not receive the spirit of bondage again to fear, but you received the Spirit of adoption by whom we cry out, "Abba, Father" (Romans 8:15).

> But when the fullness of time had come, God sent forth His Son, born of a woman, born under the law, to redeem those who were under the law, that we might receive the adoption as sons. And because you are sons, God has sent forth the Spirit of His son into your hearts, Crying out, "Abba, Father" (Galatians 4:4–6).

It is a paradox—adoption by birth/rebirth. You receive childhood from God when you cry out to Him and He enters you through your heart. And when He sent His Spirit into your heart, you were suddenly in this daddy and child relationship. The heavenly Father allowed you to enter a personal relationship with Him by the Spirit. We become children of God by rebirth or by adoption via the Holy Spirit. Regeneration also highlights the concept of being born again. The concept of regenerate, in its basic definition, includes synonyms like recreate and reproduce. If something is initially made it is created, produced, or generated. If something is made again, it is recreated, reproduced, or regenerated. Paul wrote to Titus:

> But when the kindness and the love of God our Savior toward man appeared, not by works of righteousness which we have done, but according to his mercy He saved us, through the washing of regeneration and renewing of the Holy Spirit,. . . (Titus 3:4–5).

Our salvation and spiritual childhood is obtained "through the cleansing of the new birth." (Ryrie pg. 1867).[15] The Holy Spirit regenerated, recreated, reproduced, and rebirthed us into the kingdom. The aforementioned passages about adoption and regeneration (Romans 8:15; Galatians 4:4–6; and Titus 3:4–5) are surrounded by teachings on heirship. The rebirthed, recreated, reproduced, regenerated, and spiritually adopted people are children of God.

> The Spirit Himself bears witness with our spirit that we are children of God, and if children, then heirs—heirs of God and joint heirs with Christ . . . (Romans 8:16–17).

You are the mission of the Holy Spirit! The Holy Spirit is on a mission and you are it! You are the mission field of God the Holy Spirit! He wants you to be His child, so he rebirths you, adopts you, and regenerates you into His eternal spiritual kingdom.

Think on these things. Meditate.

# Mission 26: Liberate You

You are the mission of the Holy Spirit! The Holy Spirit is on a mission and you are it! You are the mission field of God the Holy Spirit! He wants to liberate you. He wants to set you free.

We are often like the Pharisees who deny our spiritual bondage. When Jesus told those religious leaders, "the truth shall make you free," (John 8:32), they denied being enslaved. They retorted, "We are Abraham's descendants, and have never been in bondage to anyone. How can you say, 'You will be made free?'" (John 8:33). Those religious leaders only considered bondage in earthly terms and did not realize their enslavement to themselves and their religion. After Jesus pointed to their slavery to sin, He continued, "Therefore if the Son makes you free, you shall be free indeed" (John 8:36). The truth is liberating. The Son, who is the Truth, is the Lord. "Now the Lord is the Spirit, and where the Spirit of the Lord is, there is Liberty" (II Corinthians 3:17). The Holy Spirit of the Lord Jesus is in believers and sets them free. He delivers them from the judgment and death of the old covenant letter or law, liberates them from sin and the old way of life, and frees them from fears and inhibitions to serve Him. Paul wrote:

> There is therefore now no condemnation to those who are in Christ Jesus, who do not walk according to the flesh but according to the Spirit. For the law of the Spirit of life in Christ Jesus has made me free from the law of sin and death (Romans 8:1–2).

> . . . for the letter kills, but the Spirit gives life (II Corinthians 3:6b).

The Spirit sets us free from within to obey the law. He motivates and compels internally to live an externally righteous life that honors God's Word and glorifies the Lord Jesus Christ. The Spirit frees us from sin and gives victory over habits and addictions that have plagued our lives and kept us from the kingdom of God. Look at the liberating mission of God as the power of Jesus' name and the Holy Spirit set people free from their past lifestyles and sin:

> Do you not know that the unrighteous will not inherit the kingdom of God? Do not be deceived. Neither fornicators, nor idolaters, nor adulterers, nor homosexuals, nor sodomites, nor thieves, nor covetous, nor drunkards, nor revilers, nor extortioners, will inherit the kingdom of God. And such were some of you. But you were washed, but you were sanctified, but you were justified in the name of the Lord Jesus and by the Spirit of our God (I Corinthians 6:9–11).

The Holy Spirit wants you to have deliverance from and victory over your sinful lifestyle. He also wants to liberate you from your fears and inhibitions of life and service for Him. Paul told young Timothy, "For God has not given us a spirit of fear, but of power and of love, and of a sound mind" (II Timothy 1:7). The Holy Spirit who dwells in believers is not a Spirit of fear, but a Liberator from fear. He is the Spirit of love and John reminds us:

> *There is no fear in love; but perfect love casts out fear, because fear involves torment. But he who fears has not been made perfect in love (I John 4:18).*

Freedom from fear happens when we receive the perfect love of God into our lives as it is delivered to us in the person of God the Holy Spirit. My first mission trip to Liberia during their civil war included having a machine gun barrel aimed at me. The end of the barrel was approximately eight to ten inches from my ribs. An angry soldier was on the trigger end of the gun. The Holy Spirit kept me fearless and full of peace. The witch doctor over the village in India nervously paced back and forth a few feet behind me as I shared the Gospel of Jesus with the villagers. The Holy Spirit freed me from being intimidated by the witch doctor's threatening paces, and eighteen of the three hundred Indians received Christ. You are the mission of the Holy Spirit. The Holy Spirit is on a mission and you are it.

You are the mission field of God the Holy Spirit. He wants to liberate you, free you, deliver you, and give you victory from the bondage of the law, the enslavement of yourself, and the chains of sin.

Think on these things. Meditate.

# Mission 27: Renew You

Y ou are the mission of the Holy Spirit! The Holy Spirit is on a mission and you are it! You are the mission field of God the Holy Spirit! He wants to renew you—give you new life.

The ministries of God the Son and God the Holy Spirit overlap, intertwine, and complement each other as you may have noticed while focusing on these missions of the Holy Spirit. Renewal is another facet of mission that we see the Son and the Spirit are involved in ministry together. John 6:63 says: "It is the Spirit that gives life; the flesh profits nothing. The words that I speak to you are spirit, and they are life." One dynamic of this verse is the distinction of Jesus' teachings. He aimed His lessons at the spirit of an individual, so the Spirit would change his/her life. The Holy Spirit's missionary endeavor includes delivering the teachings of Jesus to our spirit to bring us renewal and new life. Paul told the Romans that ". . . we should serve in the newness of the Spirit and not in the oldness of the letter" (Romans 7:6b). The Holy Spirit brings a newness to our service to God. We are now internally motivated by the Spirit instead of externally commanded by the law. Spirit internalization and motivation result in new life.

> For those who live according to the flesh set their minds on the things of the flesh, but those who live according to the Spirit, the things of the Spirit. For to be carnally minded is death, but to be spiritually minded is life and peace. . . . And if Christ is in you, the body is dead because of sin, but the Spirit is life because of righteousness. But if the Spirit of Him who raised Jesus from the dead dwells in you, He who raised Christ from the dead will also give life to your mortal bodies through His Spirit who dwells in you. . . . For if you live according to the flesh you will die; but if by the Spirit you put to death the deeds of the body, you will live (Romans 8:5–6, 10–11, 13).

The Spirit gives new life to those who focus on and rehearse things of the Spirit in their minds. He brings new life because of His indwelling presence and resurrecting power. The same Holy Spirit that breathed life back into the mutilated carcass of Jesus Christ lives in you, if you are a believer. He inspires new thinking, new service, new actions, and new life. Jesus—the last or second Adam—is called "a life-giving spirit" (I Corinthians 15:45). Paul wrote, "Therefore, if anyone is in Christ, he is a new creation; old things have passed away; behold, all things have become new" (II Corinthians 5:17). Spiritual ministry is to renew us, bring new life, and re-create us by crucifying the old, and making us new. The Holy Spirit makes this possible. Peter echoed and reinforced these teachings of Paul when he wrote:

*For Christ also suffered once for sins, the just for the unjust, that He might bring us to God, being put to death in the flesh but made alive by the Spirit (I Peter 3:18).*

And remember the Trinitarian combination of salvation, newness, and new life as expressed in Titus.

*But when the kindness and the love of God our Savior toward man appeared, not by works of righteousness which we have done, but according to His mercy He saved us, through the washing of regeneration and renewing of the Holy Spirit, whom He poured out on us abundantly through Jesus Christ our Savior, that having been justified by His grace we should become heirs according to the hope of eternal life (Titus 3:4–7).*

You are the mission of the Holy Spirit! The Holy Spirit is on a mission and you are it! You are the mission field of God the Holy Spirit! He wants to renew and remake you so that you have new spiritual and eternal life.

Think on these things. Meditate.

# *Mission 28: Resurrect You*

Y ou are the mission of the Holy Spirit! The Holy Spirit is on a mission and you are it! You are the mission field of God the Holy Spirit! He wants to resurrect you.

The resurrection of Jesus Christ from the dead is pivotal, vital, and essential to the Christian faith.

> *But if there is no resurrection of the dead, then Christ is not risen. And if Christ is not risen, then our preaching is vain and your faith is also vain...For if the dead do not rise, then Christ is not risen. And if Christ is not risen your faith is futile; you are still in your sins! Then also those who have fallen asleep in Christ have perished (I Cor. 15:13–14, 16–18).*

Jesus' resurrection from the dead provides a faith that is true and purposeful, the reality of forgiven sins, a hope and assurance of eternity with God, and life from death. The centrality and necessity of the resurrection of Jesus is prominent in the New Testament. The New Testament is replete with teachings and references to Jesus' resurrection. Romans 8:10–11 teaches that the same Spirit that raised Christ from the dead dwells in believers. The Spirit raised Him and the Spirit raised us. I Peter 3:18 informs us that the Holy Spirit is the one who raised Jesus from the dead. The Spirit can accomplish a physical and spiritual resurrection that we can celebrate. One resurrection happens in the visible earthly existence and the other happens in the heavenlies.

The book of Ephesians contains five references to the heavenlies or heavenly places where the spiritual resurrection occurred. Ephesians 1:3 says:

> *Blessed be the God and Father of our Lord Jesus Christ, who has blessed us with every spiritual blessing in the heavenly places in Christ (Ephesians 1:3).*

God has already blessed us with every spiritual blessing that we will ever receive—in the heavenlies in Christ. Our spiritual state or position is in Christ. That is the place where the spiritual blessings have already been given to us—in the heavenly realms in Christ Jesus. It has already been accomplished. It is a completed action in the past. These spiritual blessings are already in your possession. If you are looking for the spiritual blessings in the natural, fleshy, earthly, realms, you are not going to see them.

It is like someone bought every present you will ever receive for your entire life. Every morning you wake up to a bedroom full of gifts from the most recent delivery of the presents already purchased for you. You open and enjoy them because you realize that these are your presents already paid for in full. The future gifts you will open are already purchased for you. You just do not realize what they are until you open them. In Christ Jesus, God has already poured out every blessing for you to enjoy in the heavenly places.

Ephesians 1:20 is the second reference to the heavenlies in the book of Ephesians. It speaks of God's mighty power: ". . . which He worked in Christ when He raised Him from the dead and seated Him at His right hand in the heavenly places" (Ephesians 1:20). God, by the power of His Holy Spirit, raised Christ and seated Him in the heavenly places. We understand that the Bible teaches a literal location—a particular place that Jesus was seated at the right hand of the throne of God. But Jesus is also raised up and seated in the heavenly realms. He is seated literally and spiritually in the heavenly places.

Now, look at the third use of the heavenly places in Ephesians.

> *But God, who is rich in mercy, because of His great love with which He loved us, even when we were dead in trespasses, made us alive together with Christ (by grace you have been saved), and raised us up together, and made us sit together in the heavenly places in Christ Jesus (Ephesians 2:4–6).*

Now, wait a minute! That is where Jesus is seated! When were we raised with Christ and seated with Him? You were standing, sitting, or in some physical position when you were saved by grace. But, when you received your salvation, you were raised from the dead and seated in the heavenlies in Christ. Romans 6 is all about His death being our death and His resurrection our resurrection. Galatians 2:20 says, "I have been crucified with Christ; it is no longer I who live, but Christ lives in me." Colossians 3:1–3 says:

> *If then you were raised with Christ seek those things which are above, where Christ is, sitting at the right hand of God. Set your mind on things above, not on things on the earth. For you died, and your life is hidden with Christ in God (Colossians 3:1–3).*

So, when Jesus died He was buried, He was raised from the dead, and He was seated in the heavenly places. When you became a Christian you died to yourself, the old man was crucified, you were buried with Christ, He raised you up a new person, and you were seated in the heavenly places in Christ Jesus.

Christians reading these words may be sitting in a chair in the flesh, but in the heavenlies you are seated with Christ. You were raised up by the power of the Holy Spirit to be seated in the heavenly realms with Jesus.

You are the mission of the Holy Spirit. The Holy Spirit is on a mission and you are it. You are the mission field of God the Holy Spirit. He wants to resurrect you and raise you up as He did Jesus Christ, and seat you in the heavenly places in Christ Jesus.

Think on these things. Meditate.

# Mission 29: Sanctify You

Y ou are the mission of the Holy Spirit! The Holy Spirit is on a mission and you are it! You are the mission field of God the Holy Spirit! He wants to sanctify you, purge you, purify you, and make you Holy.

God is holy! He is the Holy Spirit! He is perfect, separate, pure, consecrated, sacred—holy. He wants you to be like Him.

> *Therefore gird up the loins of your mind, be sober, and rest your hope fully upon the grace that is to be brought to you at the revelation of Jesus Christ; as obedient children, not conforming yourselves to the former lusts, as in your ignorance; but as He who called you is holy, you also be holy in all your conduct, because it is written, "Be holy, for I am Holy." (I Peter 1:13–16).*

God commands us to be holy like Him. He desires us to be holy internally (in the inner man) and externally in our conduct and lives. We do not gravitate to the Holy by ourselves. Our minds have not been thinking holy thoughts. We have been disobedient. We have conformed to the world and our lusts. We need a holy God to deliver us from all of these impurities and our fleshly lives. Praise God we have a Holy Spirit who wants to purge, purify, consecrate, perfect, and sanctify us.

God's plan from the beginning has been our sanctification. There are many facets of the sanctifying mission of the Spirit. Salvation through the sanctification of the Holy Spirit is one dynamic of His mission for our holiness.

> *But we are bound to give thanks to God always for you, brethren beloved by the Lord, because God from the beginning chose you for salvation through sanctification of the Spirit and belief in the truth (II Thessalonians 2:13).*

The Holy Spirit also sanctifies by making us acceptable to God. He sets us apart to be an offering with which God is pleased. Paul wrote:

> *That I might be a minister of Jesus Christ to the Gentiles, ministering the gospel of God, that the offering of the Gentiles might be acceptable, sanctified by the Holy Spirit (Romans 15:16).*

The sanctification of the Spirit also includes our justification. We are forgiven and separated from our sin by the sanctifying power of the Holy Spirit. After listing different sins and life styles that keep people out of God's kingdom, Paul wrote:

*And such were some of you. But you were washed, but you were sanctified, but you were justified in the name of the Lord Jesus and by the Spirit of our God (I Corinthians 6:11).*

The Spirit rebirths us, sets us apart, and separates us from our sin. We are acquitted. As we were taught in Sunday School, "Just as if I'd never sinned."

Sanctification by the Spirit also speaks to our sexual and moral purity.

*For this is the will of God, your sanctification that you should abstain from sexual immorality . . . for God did not call us to uncleanness, but in holiness. Therefore, he who rejects this does not reject man, but God, who has also given us His Holy Spirit. (I Thessalonians 4:3, 7–8).*

Many people want to know God's will for their lives. In addition to His redemptive will that people would be saved, and His will for our gratitude, we see that sanctification is His will. The context clearly shows that sexual purity is His will. A sacred sexual life is only possible by the Holy Spirit given to us.

The Holy Spirit is also active in the sanctifying blood sacrifice of Jesus that sets us apart to serve God. The Hebrew writer put it this way:

*For if the blood of bulls and goats and the ashes of a heifer, sprinkling the unclean, sanctifies for the purifying of the flesh, how much more shall the blood of Christ who through the eternal Spirit offered Himself without spot to God, purge your conscience from dead works to serve the living God? (Hebrews 9:13–14).*

The sanctifying Holy Spirit empowered Jesus to pour out His sanctifying blood, so that we would not only be purified, but we would serve Him.

Peter extended the sanctification for purity and service to every facet of our obedience. In I Peter 1:2, he wrote that the sanctification of the Holy Spirit is "for obedience." The purpose of the sanctifying ministry of the Spirit is, in part, our obedience. Additionally, concerning sanctification and obedience, Peter wrote:

*Since you have purified your souls in obeying the truth through the Spirit in sincere love of the brethren, love one another fervently with a pure heart (I Peter 1:22).*

The Holy Spirit empowers us to obey the truth which is a process for purifying our souls—our mind, will, and emotions. The sanctification of the soul man by the Spirit results in a pure and genuine love for one another.

You are the mission of the Holy Spirit! The Holy Spirit is on a mission and you are it! You are the mission field of God the Holy Spirit! He wants to sanctify you—save you, make you acceptable to God, justify you, purify you, compel you to serve God, and inspire you to live obediently in love.

Think on these things. Meditate.

# Mission 30: Secure You

Y ou are the mission of the Holy Spirit! The Holy Spirit is on a mission and you are it! You are the mission field of God the Holy Spirit! He wants to assure, secure, and seal you.

Uncertainty in life is debilitating, distractive, and unsettling for us. One of the basic truths that we want new believers to experience is assurance. We want them to know for sure that they have eternal life. Our desire is for them to know and experience the presence and power of Christ in their lives as He fulfills His promises. God the Holy Spirit makes these assurances possible for us.

The Holy Spirit moves into a person when that individual becomes a Christian. The Spirit is alive and well in the believer, doing a multitude of ministries including the assurance of salvation. "The Spirit Himself bears witness with our spirit that we are children of God" (Romans 8:16). The Holy Spirit gives an inner testimony to our spirit that we are a son or daughter of the living God. The internal voice of the Spirit is the voice of assurance, "You are My child." The remainder of the sentence tells us benefits of being children of God and reinforces assurance with the promise of glorification.

> . . . and if children, then heirs--heirs of God and joint heirs with Christ, if indeed we suffer with Him, that we may also be glorified together (Romans 8:17).

The Holy Spirit assures us, in the "now," right now, that we are God's children. Being a child of God confers heirship. Heirship determines joint heirship with Christ. Joint heirship secures our eternity in heaven. Jesus has already received His glorification, and we will be glorified with Him.

The Spirit secures our eternal inheritance in a similar manner. Look at what Paul wrote to the Ephesians:

> In Him you also trusted, after you heard the word of truth, the gospel of your salvation; in whom also, having believed, you were sealed with the Holy Spirit of promise, who is the guarantee of our inheritance until the redemption of the purchased possession, to the praise of His glory (Ephesians 1:13–14).

God the Holy Spirit is the *arrabon*.[16] He is the down payment, the earnest fee, the guarantee, that God gives to believers to secure their purchased eternal inheritance. When we buy a car or house, we make a down payment. The loan officer puts our name on the title or deed and says that it belongs to us. We have hundreds of monthly payments, but the down payment is what secures the purchase. In the earthly realms, we may miss payments and ultimately lose the car or house to the loan agency. God never defaults on this transaction. He gives us the down payment—His Spirit—to secure our inheritance, and then He seals the deal with the Holy Spirit of promise. Twice Paul echoed this message in II Corinthians:

> *Now He who establishes us with you in Christ and has anointed us is God, who also has sealed us and given us the Spirit in our hearts as a deposit (II Corinthians 1:21–22).*

> *Now He who has prepared us for this very thing is God, who also has given us the Spirit as a guarantee. Therefore, we are always confident, knowing that while we are at home in the body we are absent from the Lord. For we walk by faith, not by sight. We are confident, yes, well pleased rather to be absent from the body and to be present with the Lord (II Corinthians 5:5–8).*

The Holy Spirit has been deposited into our hearts and has sealed us to receive the inheritance promised to us. Because we are indwelt and sealed, we are confident in faith that God will keep His promise. When we die, we will leave this earthly body and be present with God in heaven. God does not give His Spirit, seal our hearts, and then take back the Spirit from us. We are His and the eternal inheritance is ours.

Right after I received the shoulder-shaking visitation of God when He called me into full-time ministry, my eyes fell on the words of I John 5:13:

> *These things I have written to you who believe in the name of the Son of God, that you may know that you have eternal life, and that you may continue to believe in the name of the Son of God (I John 5:13).*

The Holy Spirit immediately spoke to my heart, "Wade, if you are going to help other people know for sure they have eternal life, I don't want you to ever doubt it again." One of the multiple purposes of the Spirit-inspired scripture is to help a person know for sure they have eternal life—assurance of everlasting life.

At the time of my call to ministry, I didn't realize the assurances of the Spirit surrounding I John 5:13. The Spirit confirms and assures us that we abide in God and He abides in us.

> *Now he who keeps His commandments abides in Him, and He in him. And by this we know that He abides in us, by the Spirit whom He has given us (I John 3:24).*

> *"By this we know that we abide in Him, and He in us, because he has given us of His Spirit" (I John 4:13).*

Also, the Holy Spirit assures us that Jesus is the Christ, God's Messiah. Father, Son, and Spirit all testify to this truth.

> *This is He who came by water and the blood—Jesus Christ; not only by water, but by water and blood. And it is the Spirit who bears witness, because the*

*Spirit is truth. For there are three who bear witness in heaven: the Father, the Word, and the Holy Spirit; and these three are one, And there are three that bear witness on earth; the Spirit, the water, and the blood; and these three agree as one (I John 5:6–8).* [*]

The Spirit testifies in heaven and on earth that Jesus is the Christ. He proclaims the truth of Jesus' Messiahship so that you will believe it and be convinced of it in your heart. God the Holy Spirit wants to assure us of many truths. He wants to assure us of God's presence, His love, His forgiveness, His indwelling, our salvation in Him, our eternal inheritance, His abiding in us, and the truth that Jesus is the Christ.

You are the mission of the Holy Spirit! The Holy Spirit is on a mission and you are it! You are the mission field of God the Holy Spirit! He wants to assure and secure you.

Think on these things. Meditate.

---

[*] I know that people wrestle with textual issues of I John 5:6–8. There is nothing in this passage that is inconsistent with biblical truth. Inerrancy is inherent in whose word it is. It is God's Word.

# Mission 31: Sovereignly Intervene for You

You are the mission of the Holy Spirit! The Holy Spirit is on a mission and you are it! You are the mission field of God the Holy Spirit! He wants to do "God things," miraculous signs and wonders, and divine interventions in your life.

The record of the birth of Jesus as recorded in the Gospel of Matthew speaks of the sovereign and divine intervention of the Holy Spirit in the lives of Mary and Joseph.

> *Now the birth of Jesus Christ was as follows: After His Mother Mary was betrothed to Joseph, before they came together, she was found with child of the Holy Spirit. Then Joseph her husband, being a just man, and not wanting to make her a public example, was minded to put her away secretly. But while he thought about these things, behold an angel of the Lord appeared to him in a dream, saying, "Joseph, son of David, do not be afraid to take to you Mary your wife, for that which is conceived in her is of the Holy Spirit" (Matthew 1:18–20).*

The Holy Spirit caused Mary to be pregnant without physical human intercourse! God is the One who opens the womb. So, God, the Holy Spirit impregnated Mary the virgin as He sovereignly willed. She agreed to this divine intervention willingly when the angel told her about this miraculous blessing from God. Joseph received a divine intervention, which confirmed the Holy Spirit's sovereign act, and he surrendered his will to the sovereign infiltration of the Holy Spirit in his life. God the Holy Spirit's unexpected and unsolicited intervention changed the course of Mary and Joseph's lives. It changed the course of life and history for all of mankind as the Spirit sovereignly fulfilled His purpose for their lives.

The Book of Acts records numerous divine interventions of the Holy Spirit. The outpouring of the Holy Spirit at Pentecost was a sovereign act of God as Luke recorded it in Acts 2:1–4. The rushing wind, tongues of fire, and language that everyone understood is quite miraculous. In Acts 4:8ff, we see Peter was filled with the Spirit and he spoke boldly after the lame man was healed. Prayer shook the house and everyone present was filled with the Spirit and boldly proclaimed God's Word (Acts 4:31). Acts 8 records the Spirit's intervention in Philip's life. The Holy Spirit told Philip to go witness to the eunuch in the Chariot (Acts 8:29). After Philip shared Jesus with the man and baptized him, ". . . the Spirit of the Lord caught Philip away . . ."(Acts 8:39). The Holy Spirit sovereignly relocated Philip in a moment. The account and recount of the "Gentile Pentecost" in Acts 10 and 11 reveal specific interventions in the lives of Peter, Cornelius, and the people around them when the Pentecostal outpouring of the Spirit was duplicated for the Gentiles. In Acts 11:28, the Spirit revealed through Agabus that there would be a famine. Acts 13:2–4 records the Spirit selecting missionaries as He sovereignly intervened in the prayer and fasting gathering at Antioch. Paul was filled with the Spirit and spoke a curse of blindness on a sorcerer (Acts 13:9–11). No wonder some call it "The Acts of the Holy Spirit."

The rest of the New Testament documents numerous signs, wonders, miracles, divine acts, and sovereign interventions of the Holy Spirit. Healings, prophecies, resurrections, deliverances, exorcisms, and other signs, wonders, and miracles are sown throughout the New Testament. Look what we find in the Bible when things happen "in the Spirit." Read what occurred when people were enveloped by the Spirit, energized by the Spirit, and in the ecstasy of the Holy Spirit. In Matthew 22:42–45, Jesus taught that David called his future descendant "Lord" when he was "in the Spirit." The Spirit revealed to David that the Messiah would be from his lineage and gave him the inspired prophecy while he was in the Spirit. The controversial account of Mark's version of the Great Commission includes:

> *And these signs will follow these who believe: In My name they will cast out demons; they will speak with new tongues; they will take up serpents; and if they drink anything deadly, it will by no means hurt them; they will lay hands on the sick, and they will recover (Mark 16:17–18).*

Mark ended his gospel record inspired by the Spirit by saying, "And they went out and preached everywhere, the Lord working with them and confirming the word through accompanying signs. Amen" (Mark 16:20). Jesus "rejoiced in the Spirit" (Luke 10:21), when the seventy returned with the reality of spiritual victories. "Paul purposed in the Spirit (Acts 19:21)," to go to Jerusalem and Rome. He taught that circumcision was an internal matter of the heart, "in the Spirit" (Romans 2:29). Paul instructed the Romans further when he confirmed that they were "in the Spirit," which was only possible because they were indwelt (Romans 8:9). He reminded the Galatians that they had "begun in the Spirit" (Galatians 3:3), and they should continue to "walk in the Spirit and live in the Spirit" to avoid fleshly lusts (Galatians 5:16, 25). He taught the Ephesians to pray "in the Spirit" (Ephesians 6:18). It was "in the Spirit" where John was taken to hear voices, see visions, and vocalize the prophecies as he was commanded (Revelation 1:10, 4:1–2, 17:3, 21:10).

You are the mission of the Holy Spirit! The Holy Spirit is on a mission and you are it! You are the mission field of God the Holy Spirit! He wants to sovereignly intervene in your life.

Think on these things. Meditate.

# Mission 32: Speak To and Through You

You are the mission of the Holy Spirit! The Holy Spirit is on a mission and you are it! You are the mission field of God the Holy Spirit! He wants to speak to you and through you.

Jesus shared a couple of striking teachings about the Spirit speaking to and through individuals in His Matthew 10 instructions:

> *But when they deliver you up, do not worry about how or what you should speak. For it will be given to you in that hour what you should speak; for it is not you who speak, but the Spirit of your Father who speaks in you (Matthew 10:19–20).*

Messages come from God. God the Holy Spirit inspired the scriptures, so we have those messages in our possession. He also gives messages sovereignly to those who come to Him and seek out His desired proclamations. The key to homiletics, which is the study of preaching, is to seek God for His messages. He has a message for every particular group of people on every specific date. The Spirit wants to reveal and give that message to you. He wants you to share it with others. Since He is the Source of the message, He gets the glory and credit for the impact of it on people's lives. The Spirit will help us to forward and deliver the message that He gives us. Sometimes He will supernaturally speak messages through us that we have not heard before that moment. There are times when I jot down notes while I am preaching because the Spirit has me share something I had not previously heard or read. Search to discover what the Holy Spirit wants you to proclaim, and be ready for the Spirit to spontaneously speak to you and through you.

Acts includes accounts of the inspiration of the Spirit and the messages He gave to His servants. Those who disputed with Stephen about the faith, "were not able to resist the wisdom and the Spirit by which he spoke" (Acts 6:10). Ananias was given specific messages to tell Saul (Paul) when he dialogued with the Lord.

> *Arise and go to the street called Straight, and inquire at the house of Judas for one called Saul of Tarsus, for behold, he is praying. And in a vision he has seen a man named Ananias coming in and putting his hand on him, so that he might receive his sight... Go, for he is a chosen vessel of Mine to bear My name before Gentiles, kings, and the children of Israel. For I will show him how many things he must suffer for My name's sake (Acts 9:11–12, 15–16).*

The Spirit spoke to an individual to share a specific message with another particular person. He gave detailed information about "who, what, when, where, why, and how." Peter was also given a specific message concerning the men who came from Cornelius' place. The preliminaries to the Gentile Pentecost include the Holy Spirit speaking to Peter: "Behold three men are seeking you. Arise therefore, go down and go with them, doubting nothing; for I have sent them" (Acts 10:19–20). In the church at Antioch, the Holy Spirit spoke the same confirming message to five men who were fasting and praying together.

> *As they ministered to the Lord and fasted, the Holy Spirit said, "Now separate to Me Barnabas and Saul for the work to which I have called them" (Acts 13:2).*

The Spirit wants to give us messages. He wants us to receive those messages. We need to stop, pray, fast, and listen to hear what He wants us to know, do, or share with others. Many gifts of the Spirit are verbal speaking manifestations—words of wisdom, words of knowledge, prophesy, tongues, and interpretation of tongues (I Corinthians 12:8–10). There are also facets of speaking connected to other gifts. For example, one who has the gift of discerning spirits may need to inform or forewarn others once the Spirit gives discernment. The preface to the listing of spiritual gifts includes a fascinating teaching about the Holy Spirit and messages.

> *Therefore I make known to you that no one speaking by the Spirit of God calls Jesus accursed, and no one can say Jesus is Lord except by the Holy Spirit (I Corinthians 12:3).*

The Holy Spirit will never give a message that curses the Lord Jesus Christ. Nobody can genuinely say that Jesus is Lord apart from the power of the Holy Spirit. A person can say the words, "Jesus is Lord," but not in the dynamic of a believer, nor in the spirit of martyrdom. The late Dr. Fred Young illustrated this point in a seminary class with a story that went something like this:

> A Christian and a Muslim were riding together on a train in a Muslim country. The Muslim said, "I understand that you Christians believe that no one can say Jesus is Lord except by the Spirit of the Lord." The Christian responded, "That's correct." The Muslim said, "Jesus is Lord. So there." The Christian said nothing in response. They rode in silence until the Muslim got ready to depart from the train. The Christian followed him to the door and yelled to the crowd, "You Muslims come here! This man has something he wants to say to you!" The Muslim remained silent because he knew that saying "Jesus is Lord" in that setting would have cost him his life, probably at the hands of his own family.

The Spirit wants to share messages that He wants proclaimed to individuals and groups. One of the commonalities of the seven letters to the seven churches in the Revelation is the closing remark, "He who has an ear, let him hear what the Spirit says to the churches" (Revelation 2:7, 11, 17, 29, 3:6, 13, 22). Whoever has one ear in the singular. Not who has ears in the plural. The individual who has one ear, who has the capacity to hear and receive messages—listen! The Spirit is speaking messages to the churches. In addition to the seven messages to the seven churches is the future heavenly invitation:

> *And the Spirit and the bride say, "Come!" And let him who hears say, "Come!" And let him who thirsts come. And whoever desires, let him take the water of life freely (Revelation 22:17).*

You are the mission of the Holy Spirit! The Holy Spirit is on a mission and you are it! You are the mission field of God the Holy Spirit! He wants to speak to you and through you.

Think on these things. Meditate.

# Mission 33: Strengthen You

Y ou are the mission of the Holy Spirit! The Holy Spirit is on a mission and you are it! You are the mission field of God the Holy Spirit! He wants to strengthen you.

"Life verses" are those special scriptures that God uses to speak personally to our hearts and help us in life. I became acquainted with Ephesians 3:16 as one of my life verses while I was in seminary. My Monday through Thursday schedule ran from 5:00 a.m. to 10:00 p.m. once I settled into the seminary routine. After a few months of early quiet times, classes, part-time associate ministries, and a fifty-eight-mile round-trip commute, I had become tired. One morning, during my alone time with God, my tired eyes (part of my fatigued body) read these words, ". . . that He would grant you, according to the riches of His glory, to be strengthened with might through His Spirit in the inner man" (Ephesians 3:16). The instant I finished reading this verse, I experienced an "infusion." It was electric! Similar, yet, unique to experiencing a filling of the Holy Spirit, I was immediately empowered, energized, and invigorated by the indwelling Spirit. I continue to quote Ephesians 3:16 on multiple occasions. The electric physical sensation is not always experienced, but the strengthening ministry of the Spirit still occurs in my times of need. Whether I begin to get weary from everyday demands, get called out in the night, share in the sanctuary, lay block in Mexico, or battle spiritual warfare locally, in Africa, Haiti, or wherever, God the Holy Spirit is still my source of strength. It is a personal fulfillment of Isaiah 40:31:

> But those who wait on the Lord shall renew their strength; they shall mount up with wings like eagles, they shall run and not be weary, they shall walk and not faint (Isaiah 40:31).

You are the mission of the Holy Spirit! The Holy Spirit is on a mission and you are it! You are the mission field of God the Holy Spirit! He wants to strengthen you from deep within you.

Think on these things. Meditate.

# Mission 34: Teach You

You are the mission of the Holy Spirit! The Holy Spirit is on a mission and you are it! You are the mission field of God the Holy Spirit! He wants to teach you.

Four passages of scripture initially surfaced as I pondered the teaching ministry of the Holy Spirit and His desire to instruct us. First, in a list of various instructions Jesus gave to his disciples, He included these words:

> Now when they bring you to the synagogues and magistrates and authorities, do not worry about how or what you should answer, or what you should say. For the Holy Spirit will teach you in that very hour what you ought to say (Luke 12:11–12).

Last minute instruction came from the Holy Spirit to the disciples. We should constantly be praying, communing with the Spirit, and growing in our knowledge of God and His word to be prepared. But when we find ourselves in a situation to testify that is outside of our intentional generic preparations, God the Holy Spirit wants to instruct us. He will teach us what to say in those unexpected or unusual situations.

Second, the passage in John 14:26 came to mind:

> But the Helper, the Holy Spirit, whom the Father will send in My name, He will teach you all things, and bring to your remembrance all things that I said to you (John 14:26).

Jesus was known as a great teacher, even by those who did not know Him or acknowledge Him as Messiah. His opposers could never outwit Him or trap Jesus in a contradiction or falsehood. They finally quit asking Him questions because they could not refute His answers and they always ended up looking like morons. Part of the mission of the Spirit, as presented by Jesus in this verse, is to continue Jesus' teaching ministry after Christ's departure. Not only would the Holy Spirit teach new things, but He would help the disciples recall what Jesus had already taught them.

Third, the passage that surfaced was Luke's opening comments in the beginning of the Book of Acts:

> The former account I made, O Theophilus, of all that Jesus began both to do and teach until the day in which He was taken up, after He through the Holy Spirit had given commandments to the apostles whom He had chosen (Acts 1:1–2).

The Holy Spirit gave commands through Jesus to His followers before He ascended, and the Spirit continues to give commands after the ascension. It is one of the ongoing missions of the Spirit to give God's messages to people to share with others. In the past, the Holy Spirit gave the prophetic word:

> *. . . knowing this first, that no prophesy of Scripture is of any private interpretation, for prophecy never came by the will of men, but holy men of God spoke as they were moved by the Holy Spirit (II Peter 1:20–21).*

The Holy Spirit also breathed or inspired all of the scriptures. Paul wrote under the inspiration of the Holy Spirit:

> *All Scripture is given by inspiration of God, and is profitable for doctrine, for reproof, for correction, for instruction in righteousness . . . (II Timothy 3:16).*

The Holy Spirit continues to give commands for us to obey. It is part of His teaching and instructional ministry.

Fourth, the passage that came to light was I Corinthians 2:13 which says:

> *These things we also speak, not in words which man's wisdom teaches but which the Holy Spirit teaches, comparing spiritual things with spiritual (I Corinthians 2:13).*

What has not been known about God in the past has been revealed and taught to us by the Spirit. Those who have received the Spirit of God can now know the things of God's Spirit. As we reflected on I John 2:20, 27 in reference to the anointing, remember that the internal anointing, the Holy Spirit, teaches you. It is now possible to be taught spiritual things by the Spirit.

You are the mission of the Holy Spirit! The Holy Spirit is on a mission and you are it! You are the mission field of God the Holy Spirit! He is your Teacher for last-minute instructions, for teaching new things about Jesus and recalling Jesus' old teachings, for delivering God's commands to you, and for revealing spiritual things that can now be known by those who are indwelt by the Holy Spirit.

Think on these things. Meditate.

# Mission 35: Transform You

Y ou are the mission of the Holy Spirit! The Holy Spirit is on a mission field and you are it! You are the mission field of God the Holy Spirit! He wants to transform you.

The most common verse of the Bible that speaks of transformation is probably Romans 12:2 which says:

> *And do not be conformed to this world, but be transformed by the renewing of your mind, that you may prove what is that good and acceptable and perfect will of God (Romans 12:2).*

The words "conformed" and "transformed" are both imperatives or commands with middle or passive voice in the Greek.[17] Our part is not to conform to the world with the help of the Spirit, and God's part is to transform us by His Spirit. When I think of conforming, my mind pictures a doctor putting on rubber gloves that stretch and form to the shape of the physician's hands. Paul is telling the reader to not conform his/her life to the world's standards. Do not let your life be shaped by or take the shape of the world. Rather, let God transform you with a renewed mind so that you can discern and do His will. We must be yielded, surrendered, and willing for God to transform us. And, what are we being transformed from and transformed to according to Paul?

> *But we all, with unveiled face, beholding as in a mirror the glory of the Lord, are being transformed into the same image from glory to glory, just as by the Spirit of the Lord (II Corinthians 3:18).*

It is the mission of the Holy Spirit to transform you into the image of Christ. He is the true and spiritual "Transformer." The Spirit wants you and me to be changed into the image of the Lord Jesus Christ. Instead, we have tarnished and blurred the image of God in which we were originally created. Jesus is the only human who never sinned and blemished the image of God, for He was truly God and truly man. "He is the image of the invisible God . . ." (Colossians 1:15). The Holy Spirit is transforming us into the image of the Lord—Christ-likeness. The Spirit is transforming us into the image of God that He originally enjoyed with man at creation before the fall.

You are the mission of the Holy Spirit! The Holy Spirit is on a mission and you are it! You are the mission field of God the Holy Spirit! He wants to transform you into the image of Christ.

Think on these things. Meditate.

# Mission 36: Truth You

You are the mission of the Holy Spirit! The Holy Spirit is on a mission and you are it! You are the mission field of God the Holy Spirit! He wants to "truth" you.

There are some wonderfully rich teachings by Jesus about the Holy Spirit in John 14, 15, and 16. Included in these three chapters is information about God the Holy Spirit and truth. Foundationally, He is identified as "the Spirit of truth" (John 14:17, 15:26, 16:13). Truth is essential to His being because He is God. The Holy Spirit is the truth just as Jesus, God the Son, declared to be "the way, the truth, and the life" (John 14:6). Since He is the truth, the Spirit manifests truth, reveals truth, teaches truth, proclaims truth, lives truth, and wants truth to be in the lives of those He rebirths and indwells. Jesus said:

> *And I will pray the Father, and He will give you another Helper, that He may abide with you forever, even the Spirit of truth, whom the world cannot receive, because it neither sees Him nor knows Him; but you know Him, for He dwells with you and will be in you (John 14:16–17).*

Primarily, we see that the Spirit of truth indwells believers and works from the inside. He emanates truth so your conscience can become a reliable guide. He pours out truth to keep you from the deceiver and deceptions. He inspires you to tell others about Jesus known as the Truth.

> *But when the Helper comes, whom I shall send to you from the Father, the Spirit of truth who proceeds from the Father, He will testify of me (John 15:26).*

Jesus also said, "He will glorify Me, for He will take of what is Mine and declare it to you" (John 16:14). Testifying to Jesus in the power of the Holy Spirit of truth is the thrust of Acts 1:8: "But you shall receive power when the Holy Spirit has come upon you; and you shall be witnesses to Me . . ." (Acts 1:8). The Spirit of truth within believers empowers them to testify to Jesus the Truth. The third Johannine reference to the Spirit of truth is found in John 16:13:

> *However, when He, the Spirit of truth, has come, He will guide you into all truth; for He will not speak on His own authority, but whatever He hears He will speak; and He will tell you things to come (John 16:13).*

Since He is the Spirit of truth, He will guide you according to truth—the truth essential to His existence, and the truth in the scripture that He inspired—the Word of truth. He will forward messages from God, the Father of truth, and from God the Son of truth—Jesus. The Spirit will also foretell the future according to truth, since He is the prophetic source. Later, in his epistles, John simply wrote, ". . . the Spirit is truth" (I John 5:6). Applications of the Spirit of truth are seen in Paul's writings and life. He wrote:

> *For those who live according to the flesh set their minds on the things of the flesh, but those who live according to the Spirit, the things of the Spirit (Romans 8:5).*

Our thoughts are primary determiners of our lives. Fleshly, earthly, lustful thoughts are followed by fleshly, earthly, lustful lives. Spirit-focused thoughts lead to Spirit-lived lives. Lives that are lived according to the Spirit are based on truth because the Spirit is truth. Thinking about, rehearsing, and meditating on God's truths help us to live according to the Spirit.

Another Pauline application to the Spirit of truth relates to the conscience. Paul wrote, "I tell the truth in Christ, I am not lying, my conscience also bearing me witness in the Holy Spirit" (Romans 9:1). He realized that the Holy Spirit was confirming, in his conscience, that what he was writing was truth. Our conscience can potentially be a good guide, but it may not be a consistently reliable guide. The indwelling Spirit of truth can be in control of our conscience and help us to say or do the truth.

Of course, the Spirit of truth is relevant to the Word of truth, which Paul called, "the sword of the Spirit" (Ephesians 6:17). The sword is the offensive and defensive part of the full armor of God. It is used to defend against lies and false doctrine and is used to propagate and initiate truth. The Spirit and the scriptures will not violate each other because they are both truth. Truth is to be believed and lived in the power of the Holy Spirit according to God's Word.

You are the mission of the Holy Spirit! The Holy Spirit is on a mission and you are it! You are the mission field of God the Holy Spirit! He wants to "truth" you.

Think on these things. Meditate.

# Mission 37: Unify You

Y ou are the mission of the Holy Spirit! The Holy Spirit is on a mission and you are it! You are the mission field of God the Holy Spirit! He wants to unify you with other believers.

The currently unanswered prayer of Jesus is recorded in John 17 where He included this intercession for believers:

> . . . that they all may be one, as You, Father, are in Me, and I in You; that they also may be one in Us, that the world may believe that You sent Me (John 17:21).

Jesus' desire for His followers is for them to be so unified that it is like they share essential being as He and the Father are one—God the Father and God the Son. God the Holy Spirit has the unity to make Jesus' prayer become a reality.

One of the main hindrances to believers becoming unified is the misconception that the unity is *our* unity. Ephesians 4:3 says, "endeavoring to keep the unity of the Spirit in the bond of peace." It is the Spirit's unity not our unity. The Greek has it in the genitive case, which is a possessive—the Spirit's unity.[18] We are to strive to obtain and maintain a oneness that God the Holy Spirit has for us that is like the unity Jesus prayed for believers to experience.

Churches began to invite me to preach when I was eighteen years old. My first out of town invitation included an overnight at a farm house with folks I had never met. Toward the end of the evening I learned that the church I would be preaching at the next morning recently had a split. I was horrified because I only had notes for one sermon with me and it was on Ephesians 4:1–6:

> I, therefore, the prisoner of the Lord, beseech you to have a walk worthy of the calling with which you were called, with all lowliness and gentleness, with longsuffering, bearing with one another in love, endeavoring to keep the unity of the Spirit in the bond of peace. There is one body and one Spirit, just as you were called in one hope of your calling; one Lord, one faith, one baptism; one God and Father of all, who is above all, and through all, and in you all (Ephesians 4:1–6).

I did not sleep well that night, concerned that the congregation would think I knew of the split before I came to share with them. I assumed that the congregation would feel that I targeted them and was making an issue of their disunity. How would you respond to an eighteen-year-old itinerant preacher still using "Sea Breeze" to fight pimples? By the Grace of God it all turned out well, and I learned two powerful primary lessons about unity in the church. First, God prizes unity in the Body as an extremely high priority. Second, it is the Spirit's unity that we endeavor to keep with fellow believers.

Just as the fruit of the Spirit (love, joy, peace, etc.) exists when the Holy Spirit is present and in control, so also, the unity of the Spirit naturally exists when He is present and in control. We do not normally produce the spiritual fruit and we do not naturally have the unity of the Spirit. We have to intentionally be yielded to the presence and ministry of the Spirit to experience what He naturally does in light of His person, character, and attributes. Just because we are indwelt by the Spirit, does not mean we automatically produce the fruit of the Spirit, nor have the unity of the Spirit. We are one in Christ in the heavenlies. But the oneness of the Spirit is an endeavor we must do to keep the unity of the Spirit on the earth.

In the construction terminology of Ephesians 2:19–22, we see God bringing together individual believers, "for a habitation of God in the Spirit" (Ephesians 2:22). In the giving of spiritual gifts we see these teachings:

> *Now there are diversities of gifts, but the same Spirit…one and the same Spirit works all these things, distributing to each one individually as He wills…For by one Spirit we were all baptized into one body…But now indeed there are many members, yet one body…there should be no schism in the body, but that the members should have the same care for one another (I Corinthians 12:4, 11, 13, 20, 25).*

In the same physical language Paul wrote about our unity of the faith (Ephesians 4:13) saying:

> *…from whom the whole body, joined and knit together by what every joint supplies, according to the effective working by which every part does its share, causes growth of the body for the edifying of itself in love (Ephesians 4:16).*

Wherever the Holy Spirit is present and involved, whether the body or spiritual gifts, He is about unity. He is the Spirit of unity. He promotes His unity, which He exhibits with God the Father and God the Son. The Spirit desires this unity for us and makes it possible for believers to experience His unity.

You are the mission of the Holy Spirit! The Holy Spirit is on a mission and you are it! You are the mission field of God the Holy Spirit! He wants to unify you.

Think on these things. Meditate.

# Mission 38: Walk You

Y ou are the mission of the Holy Spirit! The Holy Spirit is on a mission and you are it! You are the mission field of God the Holy Spirit! He wants you to walk in Him—walk in the Spirit.

The new covenant prophecy of Ezekiel 36:27 says, "I will put My Spirit within you and cause you to walk in My statutes, and you will keep My judgments and do them" (Ezekial36:27).Obedience to God happens when the Holy Spirit is internalized within the believer and compels that individual to obey God's Word. The Christian spiritual journey is identified as a "walk in the Spirit." Paul taught about walking in the Spirit in his various letters. To the Romans he wrote:

> *There is therefore now no condemnation to those who are in Christ Jesus, who do not walk according to the flesh, but according to the Spirit (Romans 8:1).*

A walk in the Spirit is a condemnation-free stroll. Condemnation is not for believers. It is for unbelievers as Jesus taught Nicodemus:

> *For God did not send His Son into the world to condemn the world, but that the world through Him might be saved. He who believes in Him is not condemned; but he who does not believe is condemned already because he has not believed in the name of the only begotten Son of God (John 3:17–18).*

Believers are not condemned. Unbelievers are condemned. The Incarnation of Christ was not to condemn us, but to deliver us from the condemnation of our sin.

> *. . . He condemned sin in the flesh, that the righteous requirement of the law might be fulfilled in us who do not walk according to the flesh, but according to the Spirit (Romans 8:3–4).*

The walk in the Spirit is a holy and righteous journey made possible by the perfect and sacrificial life of Jesus. Paul's concern for the spiritual direction of the Galatians is found in a series of questions:

> *This only I want to learn from you: Did you receive the Spirit by the works of the law, or by the hearing of faith? Are you so foolish? Having begun in the Spirit, are you now being made perfect by the flesh?. . . Therefore He who supplies the Spirit to you and works miracles among you, does He do it by the works of the law, or by the hearing of faith? (Galatians 3:2–3,5).*

Walking in the Spirit is a walk of faith. You receive the Holy Spirit by faith and you continue to trust in Him by faith. Later, in Galatians 5:16–25, Paul pointed out the conflict and the distinctions between the walk in the Spirit and the walk in the flesh.

> *Walk in the Spirit, and you shall not fulfill the lust of the flesh. For the flesh lusts against the Spirit, and the Spirit against the flesh; and these are contrary to one another, so that you do not do the things that you wish. But if you are led by the Spirit, you are not under the law. Now the works of the flesh are evident, which are: adultery, fornication, uncleanness, . . . those who practice such things will not inherit the kingdom of God. But the fruit of the spirit is love, joy, peace . . . If we live in the spirit, let us also walk in the Spirit (Galatians 5:16–19, 21b, 22a, 25).*

The spiritual walk is the Spirit-inspired life that follows our rebirth, not a fleshly lust-charged lifestyle. The walk in the Spirit is a fruitful journey not an unhealthy destructive existence. Walking in the Spirit is an eternal kingdom walk, not a temporal earthly walk that fails to inherit God's' kingdom.

The principle of reaping and sowing is relevant to walking in the Spirit. "For he who sows to his flesh will of the flesh reap corruption, but he who sows to the Spirit will of the Spirit reap everlasting life" (Galatians 6:8). After the Spirit indwells you, keep planting and consuming the things of the Spirit, so they will come out in your life. Sow to the Spirit and not the flesh and you will reap eternal spiritual blessings and life. Planting God's Word and things of the Spirit in you, gives the Spirit more seed to multiply and increase produce from you. Peter's version of the reaping and sowing principle reveals that the spiritual walk is a purifying obedience in love. He wrote:

> *Since you have purified your souls in obeying the truth through the Spirit in sincere love of the brethren, love one another fervently with a pure heart, having been born again, not of corruptible seed but incorruptible, through the word of God which lives and abides forever (I Peter 1:22–23).*

Walking in the Spirit includes the dynamics of God's Word, obedience, freedom from condemnation, holiness, righteousness, faith, Spirit-inspired living, fruitful existence, the kingdom, eternity, reaping, and sowing to the Spirit.

You are the mission of the Holy Spirit! The Holy Spirit is on a mission and you are it! You are the mission field of God the Holy Spirit! He wants you to walk in Him.

Think on these things. Meditate.

# Mission 39: Witness To and Through You

Y ou are the mission of the Holy Spirit! The Holy Spirit is on a mission and you are it! You are the mission field of God the Holy Spirit! He wants to witness to and through you.

One reason that many Christians do not experience God the Holy Spirit in their lives is because they do not witness. If someone is going to get born of the Spirit or born again, guess who is going to be present? Jesus' last words before His ascension were these:

> But you shall receive power when the Holy Spirit has come upon you and you shall be witnesses to Me in Jerusalem, and in all Judea and Samaria, and to the end of the earth (Acts 1:8).

A primary purpose of the Holy Spirit was to give power to Jesus' disciples to bear witness to Christ. If you rely on your own power, you will not testify to Jesus. If you yield to God the Holy Spirit, He will empower you to witness. When He who indwells you empowers you to witness, He will be present when someone is rebirthed or born again. The Spirit wants to witness to you and through you.

The apostles were imprisoned for witnessing, but an angel miraculously released them during the night. So they returned to the temple and resumed their teaching about Jesus. When they were arrested again for testifying about Jesus, they spoke these words as their defense:

> We ought to obey God rather than men. The God of our fathers raised up Jesus whom you murdered by hanging on a tree. Him God has exalted to His right hand to be Prince and Savior, to give repentance to Israel and forgiveness of sins. And we are His witnesses to these things, and so also is the Holy Spirit whom God has given to those who obey Him (Acts 5:29–32).

The Holy Spirit empowered the apostles to share the message of Jesus' crucifixion, and the Spirit testified to the listeners a witness to Christ. The Spirit witnessed through the apostles to the audience. He attested to the apostles' message in the hearts of the hearers.

When Paul met the Ephesian elders at Miletus, he rehearsed his ministry to them and foretold the Spirit's involvement in his future. His final words included the following:

> . . . testifying to Jews, and also to Greeks, repentance toward God and faith toward our Lord Jesus Christ. And see, now I go bound in the spirit to Jerusalem, not knowing the things that will happen to me there, except that the Holy Spirit testifies in every city, saying that chains and tribulations await me (Acts 20:21–23).

The witness of the Spirit to Paul and other believers was the same in every city. He would be imprisoned and suffer for telling others about Jesus.

The internal witness of the Spirit verified the truth of Paul's message in Romans 9:1, "I tell the truth in Christ, I am not lying: my conscience also bearing me witness in the Holy Spirit" (Romans 9:1). Internally, Paul's conscience and the Holy Spirit confirmed to him that what he said was true. The external witness of the Spirit to others was realized when Paul reassured his listeners of the Spirit's internal verification of truth. The Spirit told Paul that his conscience was accurate and his message was true. The audience could believe Paul's message to them because he verbalized the truth of the Spirit's internal witness.

Paul also reminded the Romans that the Holy Spirit gives an inner testimony to believers that they are God's kids. He wrote, "The Spirit Himself bears witness with our spirit that we are children of God" (Romans 8:16). The Spirit witnesses to our spirit the confirming assurance that we are God's children. The voice of assurance is the voice of the Spirit to believe when we are given any other message. The "familiarity factor" is getting so familiar with the voice of the Spirit to our spirit in assurance that we recognize His voice when we hear other messages and words of witness.

In his introduction to spiritual gifts, Paul inserted these words of total reliance on the Holy Spirit and the dynamics of witness to the Lordship of Christ.

> *Therefore I make known to you that no one speaking by the Spirit of God calls Jesus accursed, and no one can say that Jesus is Lord except by the Holy Spirit (I Corinthians 12:3).*

The spiritual gifts are given to believers by the Spirit. As the Spirit will not proclaim Jesus is a curse, so spiritual gifts will not be used to denounce Christ. As the Spirit is the only One who can restrain us from cursing Jesus, so also He is the only One who can cause us to genuinely testify that Jesus is Lord. The Holy Spirit witnesses to us and through us the Lordship of Jesus Christ. Similarly, Paul wrote to the Thessalonians:

> *For our gospel did not come to you in word only, but also in power, and in the Holy Spirit and in much assurance, as you know what kind of men we were among you for your sake (I Thessalonians 1:5).*

Paul's witnessing to the Corinthians included information and manifestation of the Spirit as a witness to Christ.

> *And I, brethren, when I came to you, did not come with excellence of speech or of wisdom declaring to you the testimony of God. For I determined not to know anything among you except Jesus Christ and Him crucified. I was with you in weakness, in fear, and in much trembling. And my speech and my preaching were not with persuasive words of human wisdom, but in demonstration of the Spirit and of power (I Corinthians 2:1–4).*

Paul shared the gospel of Jesus in power when the Holy Spirit came upon him. The writer of Hebrews shares about the witness of the Spirit in two distinct places. In Hebrews 2:3–4 he raises the question:

> *How shall we escape if we neglect so great a salvation, which at the first began to be spoken by the Lord, and was confirmed to us by those who heard Him, God also bearing witness both with signs and wonders with various miracles and gifts of the Holy Spirit, according to His own will? (Hebrews 2:3–4)*

The supernatural manifestations and gifts of the Spirit are witnesses that God used to confirm the message of salvation that Jesus and His followers taught. Spiritual gifts and miracles have multiple purposes including the function of testifying to the truth of salvation through Jesus. Later the Hebrew writer recorded that the Holy Spirit not only confirmed Jesus' message of salvation, but the Spirit also testified to our sanctification:

> *For by one offering he has perfected forever those who are being sanctified. And the Holy Spirit also witnesses to us; for after He had said before, "This is the covenant that I will make with them after those days, says the Lord: I will put My laws into their hearts, and in their minds I will write them," then He adds, "Their sins and their lawless deeds I will remember no more? (Hebrews 10:14–17).*

The message of the New Covenant includes the testimony of the Holy Spirit of our sanctification through internalization and complete forgiveness. John wrote about the testifying ministry of the Spirit to Jesus when he said:

> *This is He who came by water and blood—Jesus Christ; not only by water, but by water and blood. And it is the Spirit who bears witness, because the Spirit is truth. For there are three who bear witness in heaven: the Father, the Word, and the Holy Spirit; and these three are one. And there are three that bear witness on earth; the Spirit, the water, and the blood; and these three agree as one (I John 5:6–8).*

The Spirit, who is truth, gives an honest witness to Jesus Christ. Jesus is the One who lived on earth and was baptized, crucified, and resurrected according to the Spirit. Jesus is the One who now lives in heaven and He shares oneness with the Father and the Holy Spirit as the Spirit testifies. The Holy Spirit continues to witness to Jesus on the earth with the three-fold testimony of the Spirit, the water, and the blood. The Spirit continues to bear witness to and through us concerning the truths about Jesus, internal confirmations, assurances, gifting, and our sanctification.

You are the mission of the Holy Spirit! The Holy Spirit is on a mission and you are it! You are the mission field of God the Holy Spirit! He wants to witness to you and through you.

Think on these things. Meditate.

# Mission 40: Help You Not Sin Against Him

You are the mission of the Holy Spirit! The Holy Spirit is on a mission and you are it! You are the mission field of God the Holy Spirit! He wants to keep you from sinning against Him.

There are numerous sins against God the Holy Spirit recorded in the New Testament. You can blaspheme or speak against Him, receive another spirit instead of Him, grieve Him, quench Him, reject Him, insult Him, lie to Him, test or tempt Him, and generally violate Him by disobedience. The Spirit is on a mission to keep you from these sins as much as He endeavors to bring the thirty-nine positive things into your life. So, in a sense, you could say that He is on a mission to keep you from sin and violating God.

The blasphemy of the Holy Spirit is the most vile sin against the Spirit with unforgivable eternal consequences. The three Synoptic Gospels all quote Jesus' words about the blasphemy against the Spirit. Matthew's and Mark's accounts run parallel and are more detailed than Luke's one verse record of this sin against the Spirit. The context of the sin of blasphemy is the accusation of the Pharisees who determined that Jesus was casting out demons by the power of Beelzebub rather than by the Spirit of God. Denying the work of the Holy Spirit and attributing the power to a different source is blasphemous. Jesus said:

> *Therefore I say to you, every sin and blasphemy will be forgiven men, but the blasphemy against the Holy Spirit will not be forgiven men. Anyone who speaks a word against the Son of Man, it will be forgiven him; but whoever speaks against the Holy Spirit, it will not be forgiven him, either in this age or the age to come (Matthew 12:31–32).*

> *. . . but he who blasphemes against the Holy Spirit never has forgiveness, but is subject to eternal condemnation (Mark 3:29).*

Blasphemy is unforgivable. It is a sin of unbelievers leading to damnation and eternal separation from God. Giving Satan credit for the work of the Spirit and speaking against or evil of the Spirit leads to condemnation. Responding to the Holy Spirit in blasphemous ways leads to the epitome of blasphemy—rejecting Jesus Christ as Lord and Savior—and that is unforgivable.

The sin of lying to the Holy Spirit is found in Acts 5:3 in the account of Ananias and his wife Sapphira. They joined others in selling land and possessions to make sure that fellow Christians had their needs met. But, Ananias and Sapphira lied about the amount of the sale of their land. When this was discovered, Peter said:

*Ananias, why has Satan filled your heart to lie to the Holy Spirit and keep back part of the price of the land for yourself? You have not lied to men but to God (Acts 5:3, 4b).*

Ananias died on the spot. Approximately three hours later, not knowing about her husband's death, Sapphira repeated the lie about the price of the land sale. Peter said to her:

*How is it that you have agreed together to test the Spirit of the Lord? Look, the feet of those who have buried your husband are at the door, and they will carry you out (Acts 5:9).*

Sapphira died, too. This time, Peter referred to the couple's sin as testing or tempting the Spirit. The consequences for lying and testing the Spirit were severe, but because they were believers they still went to heaven. They didn't have the unforgiveness and condemnation of blasphemy against the Holy Spirit.

Another sin against the Holy Spirit that He does not want you to commit is resistance. Stephen said to the religious leaders that accused him of blasphemy: "You stiff-necked and uncircumcised in heart and ears! You always resist the Holy Spirit; as your fathers did, so do you" (Acts 7:51). The religious leaders over the centuries were best known for resisting the messages of the prophets. They had the prophets persecuted and killed. Their most recent victim was the prophet from Nazareth—Jesus. They resisted His teachings and ministry like previous prophets and, eventually, they falsely accused Him and nailed Him to a cross.

Second Corinthians 11:4 identifies what I would include as a sin against the Spirit, even though the phraseology does not specifically label it a sin against the Holy Spirit. Paul wrote:

*For if he who comes preaches another Jesus whom we have not preached, or if you receive a different spirit which you have not received, or a different gospel which you have not accepted, you may well put up with it (II Corinthians 11:4).*

I am sure, among other things, that the Holy Spirit does not want you to receive a different spirit. Deception, like in the Garden of Eden, is the stumbling block that causes us to make the wrong choices and sin. Just as deception led to sin in the garden, the deceiver can cause us to consider the wrong choice and we disobey.

Because the Holy Spirit is a person, He can be saddened or grieved. Paul wrote to the Ephesians: "And do not grieve the Holy Spirit of God, by whom you were sealed for the day of redemption" (Ephesians 4:30). This is a pointed command. He is God the Holy Spirit. The Holy Spirit is God. Do not speak, act, or live in any way that would sadden God and grieve the Spirit.

Paul was also straightforward in telling the Thessalonians, "Do not quench the Spirit" (I Thessalonians 5:19). Quenching is any way we stop or reduce the work and flow of the Holy Spirit. A wide variety of drinks are on the market to quench your thirst. The Spirit wants to flow fully and freely without limitation. Our sins, our lack of prayer, our absence of quiet time, and our distraction of hobbies and habits can all restrict or quench the Spirit.

First Thessalonians 4:7–8 mentions another sin that does not have the phrase, "sin against the Spirit," but it appears to be another violation against the Spirit. Writing about the topic of sexual immorality, Paul wrote:

> *For God did not call us to uncleanness, but in holiness. Therefore he who rejects this does not reject man, but God, who has also given us His Holy Spirit (I Thessalonians 4:7–8).*

When we reject the Spirit-inspired teachings on sexual morality and give in to sexual impurity, it is not only a sin with that person, but a rejection of God who gave us His Spirit.

Lastly, we can sin against the Holy Spirit by not keeping His word and standards. Causing discord and division among believers, not witnessing, not letting His peace rule in our hearts, or not living the fruit of the Spirit are sins against the Spirit who wants the opposite in our lives—unity, peace, and fruitfulness. These various violations against the Spirit will have consequences, yet forgiveness and grace are always available to you.

You are the mission of the Holy Spirit! The Holy Spirit is on a mission and you are it. You are the mission field of God the Holy Spirit. He wants to keep you from sinning against Him and violating God.

Think on these things. Meditate.

# Epilogue

Y ou are the mission of the Holy Spirit! The Holy Spirit is on a mission and you are it! You are the mission field of God the Holy Spirit! He has numerous things He wants to do in your life and many things He does not want in your life. I pray that God helps us to be yielded and surrendered to the Holy Spirit. He will accomplish His missions in us, if we trust Him to complete them.

"You are God's field" (I Corinthians 3:9). You are His mission field. I pray that you will more fully experience the Holy Spirit's reality and intervention in your life as you meditate on the missions of the Spirit and savor the songs.

To God be the glory!

In Him,
Wade

# End Notes

[1] Barclay M. Newman, Jr., *A Concise Greek-English Dictionary of the New Testament*. United Bible Societies 1971. Pg. 130.

[2] Ibid. Pg. 84.

[3] Ibid. Pg. 130.

[4] Wade C. Graber, *Obedience*. Pg. 17 First Printing.

[5] Charles Caldwell Ryrie, *The Ryrie Study Bible NKJV*. Moody Press 1985. Pg 132.

[6] *Webster's New Universal Unabridged Dictionary*. Random House Publishing, Inc. 1996 and Barnes & Noble Publishing, Inc. 2003 edition. Pg. 165.

[7] W. E. Vine, *Vine's Expository Dictionary of New Testament Words*. Macdonald Publishing Company. Pg. 209.

[8] Barbara and Timothy Friberg, Editors, *Analytical Greek New Testament*. Baker Book House 1981. Pp. 574 and 604.

[9] Ibid. Pg. 598.

[10] Op.cit. Vine. Pg. 903.

[11] George Ricker Berry, *Interlinear Greek-English New Testament*. Broadman Press 1980. Pg. 6.

[12] Ibid. Pg. 89.

[13] Ibid. Pg. 158.

[14] Op. cit. Vine. Pg.603.

[15] Op. cit. Ryrie. Pg. 1867.

[16] Op. cit. Vine. Pg. 351.

[17] Op. cit. Friberg, Editors. Pg. 499.

[18] Ibid. Pg. 594.

# BONUS MATERIAL

# Synopsis of Songs

**Worship MRI** came to me while I was in an MRI tube. I fell down the stairs early one morning on my way to having a quiet time. I injured my left shoulder and could not get full use or free from the pain. As a drummer, I was actually enjoying the diverse rhythms of the MRI machine. I heard myself singing a song that was new to me. The person monitoring the MRI spoke through the intercom, "Mr. Graber, are you all right?" I responded, "Yeah, I'm great!" How could I not be fine when the Holy Spirit had just given me a new song?

**God Exists** is a song that God gave me in a hotel room while I was simply contemplating Him. I was staying at a hotel for an out of town wedding. Alone in the room, God gave me this novel song with Trinitarian lyrics and a nontraditional style of music to present the Godhead.

**Celebrate the Spirit** was given to me when Steve Butler and I were selecting songs for a worship service in Ark City. We were trying to find a lively Holy Spirit song. Since Steve is an amazing musician, I said, "Why don't you just write one?" He was headed to the music library to double check if we had overlooked any songs. The Holy Spirit gave me this praise chorus at that moment, and I yelled for Steve to come hear it and write it down (because I don't know how to read or write music). We had the song for that Sunday.

**Slow Me Down, Lord,** as you might obviously suspect, hit me when I needed to slow down and make sure I was having quiet times and hearing from God. It is so easy to go 90 m.p.h. in life and get too busy to live and be at the center of God's will for you.

**Here I Stand** is an old song from college days. Peggy, my wife, was studying about Martin Luther in History of Civilization class and I was reading about him in Church History. After posting his ninety-five theses on the Castle Church door in Wittenberg, Germany, he was put on trial because of his charges against the church. I was moved by the simplicity of a line within his defense, "Here I stand; I can do no other, so help me God. Amen."

**We Know You Are With Us** came to me driving down the road in our family minivan. We were returning home from seeing our son Evan at college in Arkansas (John Brown University). The presence of the Lord began to be very powerful to me. I had Peggy write down the words as we drove. I kept rehearsing the tune for the last two hours of the trip, so I would remember it. I made a cassette of the song so Steve could write the music at a later date.

**I Love Your Company** is a re-write of a secular song entitled, "I Need Your Company" by my friend Woody (Thomas Woodworth). Woody and my brother Gary were five years older than me and let me drum for them. In the 70s, we had a band called "Pleasure" and played for Frank Pooler (manager for The Carpenters, etc.). Woody gave me permission to revamp his song for this project. New lyrics came and his old tune came to mind as I was focused on communing with God the Holy Spirit.

**Declare My Love for You** came to me during an airplane flight. I believe it was originally written on an airline napkin. There was nothing unusual about the trip. I was just communing with the Lord when the Holy Spirit gave me an extra measure of love for God that came from deep within me.

**How Long** is one of the songs the Lord gave me while I was plunking around on the piano. (You can tell that I'm a drummer by the way I play the piano.) Other songs have come to me while I have been strumming away on the guitar. Whether singing, plunking, or strumming, when the songs come to me I try to get them in some kind of form that a real musician can write them down for others to sing.

**Keep on Being Filled** was originally written by my brother Gary after the years of writing secular music and idolizing the Beatles. I asked Gary's permission to change some lyrics to fit this project. I noticed that nobody in the Bible boasts about being Spirit-filled. I have also observed that many rehearse the exhortation to be filled with the Spirit, but do not rehearse being filled with the Holy Spirit. The new lyrics acknowledge the command to be filled and rehearse being filled with the Spirit.

**Holy Spirit, Intercede** is a song that God gave me while I was strumming on the guitar and contemplating Romans 8:26. It was an awesome experience to receive the song, sing about the Spirit's intercessions, and then silently sense that the Holy Spirit was interceding for me that very moment.

**You Live in Me** is the song of my heart. Based on I Corinthians 3:16 and 6:19, it has become a living reality that my body is the Holy Spirit's temple and He lives deep inside of me. I think that God laid a foundation for this in my heart years ago when my family sang a song entitled, "My Cathedral." The teaching and example of Juan Carlos Ortiz from my college days has also helped this biblical truth become a personal reality for me.

**Speak to Me** is a song that the Holy Spirit gave to Steve Butler the verses and to me, the chorus. Glenn Shepard of International Prayer Ministries was our revivalist and Steve was our guest worship leader at First Baptist Church in El Dorado, KS. While Glenn was preaching about the ways God speaks to us, the Spirit gave Steve a song, which he wrote down as Glenn spoke. At the time of response, I felt a strong urge to drop to my knees and pray. I heard myself singing a new song—a phrase over and over again. Steve began to play the piano and accompany me. When the service ended, Steve told me about God giving him the song during the message. He was contemplating a chorus for the song, and when he heard me singing, he knew that the Holy Spirit had given me the chorus for his song.

# Worship M.R.I.

Wade Graber

♩ = 120

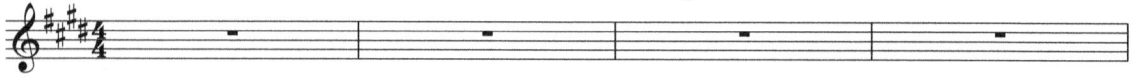

God, three in one,_____ we wor - ship_ You._____

Fath - er, Son, Spir - it,_____ we wor - ship_ You.

Three in one, ho - ly Lord._____

**Simile Chords**

God the Fath - er,_____ we wor - ship_ You._____

___ Fath - er, Son, Spir - it,_____ we wor - ship_ You._____

___ God the Fath - er, ho - ly Lord._____

God the Son,_____ we

wor - ship_ You._____ Fath - er, Son, Spir - it,_____ we

37
wor - ship_ You._____ God the Son, ho - ly Lord._____

41
___ God the Spir - it,_____

45
___ we wor - ship_ You._____ Fath - er Son, Spir - it_____

49
___ we wor - ship_ You._____ God the Spir it, ho - ly

53
Lord._____ our

57
D/E    E    D/E    E    (Sing 3x)
God ex - ists as three_ in one, Fath - er, Ho - ly Spir - it, Son.  our

59
D/E    E    D/E    E
God ex - ists as three_ in one, Fath - er, Ho - ly Spir - it, Son. We wor- ship_ You._____ We

63
wor - ship_ You._____ We wor - ship_ You._____ We

67
wor - ship__ You._____ We wor - ship You!

# God Exists

Wade Graber

Lyrics:

God ex - ists__ as Fath - er, Son and Spir - it. God ex - ists__ as Fath - er, Son and Spir - it. It's ess- ent - ial to our faith, it's what we be- lieve, a sure foun - da - tion of Chris - ti - an - i - ty. This bib - li - cal truth, this Trin - i - ty,__ it's as vi - tal as Je - sus' De - i - ty.__

# Celebrate the Spirit

Wade Graber

43 Bb/F  F  F  Gm  C  F  Bb  F

sanc-tu - a - ry, Wor-ship the Spir-it in the house of_ the Lord, Wor-ship the Spir-it in the Ho-ly_ of Ho - lies,

48 F  C7  Bb  C  F C/E Dm C Bb  C  F

you are_ the tem - ple_ of God. you are_ the tem - ple_ of God. you are_ the tem ple_ of God.

# Slow Me Down, Lord

Wade Graber

♩ = 127

Slow me down___ Lord, I want to hear Your voice.

Slow me down___ Lord, I need to hear Your voice.___ Slow me down___ Lord, I

have to hear Your voice.___ Slow me down___ Lord, I want to hear,___ I want to hear___ from You.

*similie*

Slow me down___ Lord, from rush-ing in___ this place.___

Slow me down___Lord, to know Your warm___ em - brace.___ Slow me down___Lord, to the

Ho - ly Spir - it's pace.___ Slow me down___ Lord, I want to hear,___ I want to hear from You.___

Instrumental (X5) Last time gradual slowing down   ♩=98

Slow me down___ Lord, and free me from des - pair.

Slow me down___ Lord, to know Your lov - ing care.___ Slow me down___ Lord, to

55
know that You are there.— Slow me down Lord, I want to hear,— I want to hear from You.

61
*espress.*  F⁹  E♯⁹  F⁹
I want to hear from You,— want it clear from You,

68  E♯⁹  Dm  E⁷  Am  Em  F⁹  E♯⁹  (opt. vamp)
— slow me down Lord, I want to hear from You._____

# Here I Stand

Wade Graber

♩ = 60

Here I stand, what else can I do? Here I___ am,_____ wait-ing Lord for You._ So take my

___ hand,_____ and draw me close to You. I___ need Your pres-ence,

I___ need Your guid-ance, I need Your love to see me through. What I am, in com-

par-i-son to You is mere-ly___ man,_____ with sin, and dest-i-tute._ Yet what's the___ plan,_____ You

have for me to do?_ I___ need Your pres-ence, I___ need Your guid-ance,

I need Your love to see me through. You will al-ways lead me please help me to trust, more com

- plete-ly___ for_ that is a must. Sup-er - cede_me,_ and my self-ish lust. Grant e-tern-i-ty,____ for

You are_ just._ I___ need Your pres-ence, I___ need Your guid-ance, I need Your love_ to see me

2

through.    I__ need Your pres-ence,    I__ need Your guid-ance,    I__ need Your pow-er,

I__ need Your Spir-it,    I need Your love__ to see me through.

# We Know You Are with Us

Wade Graber

Ho - ly Spir - it, we know You are with__ us,

be-cause You in- dwell__ us, be-cause of Your prom - ise. When two or more are
We don't have to beg You,

gath-ered in Your__ name, we know You are with__ us, Spir-it of__ God.
or plea for Your pre - sence,

You're al-ways with us,_____ You're om-ni-pres - ent,_____ You'll nev-er leave us!_

__ Ho - ly Spir - it, we know You are with__ us, be-cause You in- dwell__ us,

be-cause of Your prom - ise. When two or more are gath-ered in Your__ name, we know You are with_____ us, Spir-it of_____ God. We know You are

with us,_____ We know You are with us,_____ Spir-it of God!_____

# I Love Your Company

**Original music and lyrics by:**
**Tom Woodworth**
*New lyrics by:*
**Wade C. Graber**

♩ = 152

AMaj7    DMaj7    AMaj7         FMaj7  E7  AMaj7              DMaj7

You are the One,      You are God's on - ly   Son. You came to die,___
You dwell in me,      Spir-it - ual lib - er - ty.   Fel - low-ship sweet,_

7  AMaj7         FMaj7  E7  AMaj7  FMaj7              CMaj7         FMaj7

and rose a - gain   on   high.      You suf - fered on  Cal - v'ry___  for all my_
com - fort-ing Par - a - clete.     Deep sweet comm - un - ion___  with my soul_

13  CMaj7    FMaj7         CMaj7         Gm         F/A         Gm

sins.      You sent Your Spir-it___ to re - side___ deep in - side me,___  I'm___thrilled You
man.      Strength-en and help me___ grac ious God,___ Great I   Am,___

19  D      Em         D/F#      G    G/A    D sus    D         FMaj7

live   in   me,   I   love  Your   com - pa - ny.___              You live with

26  CMaj7         FMaj7         CMaj7    FMaj7         CMaj7              Gm

in   me, ___      Spir - it  and   Lord.      I know You hear me___ when I   whis - per so

32  F/A              Gm              D              Em

soft - ly___         I'm      thrilled You  live    in    me,    I

36  D/F#              G    G/A         D

love   Your   com - - pa - ny.___

# *Declare My Love for You*

Wade Graber

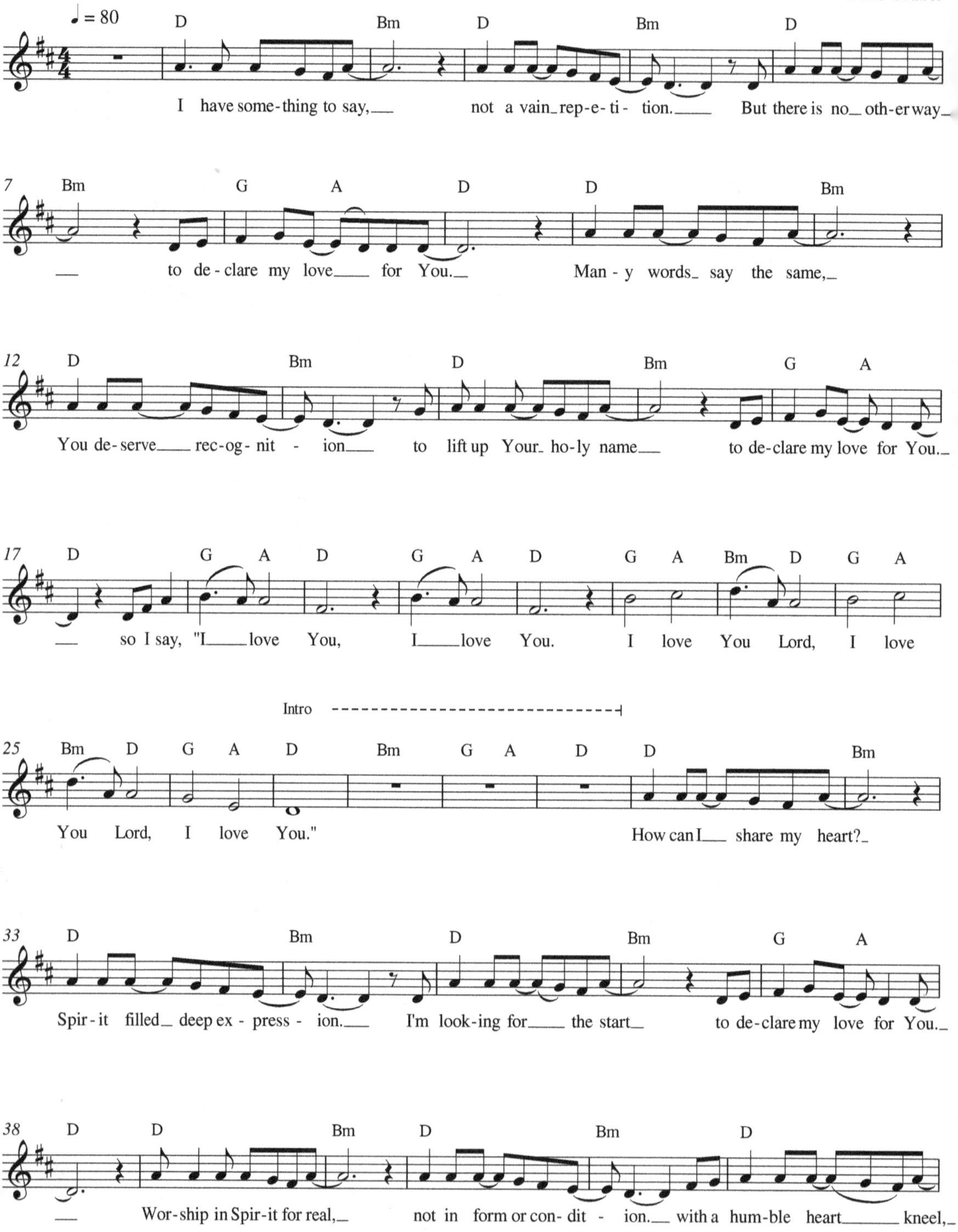

44
Bm G A D G A D G A D
to de-clare my love for You. so I say, "I love You, I love You.
51
G A Bm D G A Bm D G A 1. D Bm D Bm D
I love You Lord, I love You Lord, I love You."
60
D Bm G A D 2. D G A D G A
so I say, You, I love You, I love
68
D Bm D Bm D D Bm G A D
You."

# *How Long?*

Wade Graber

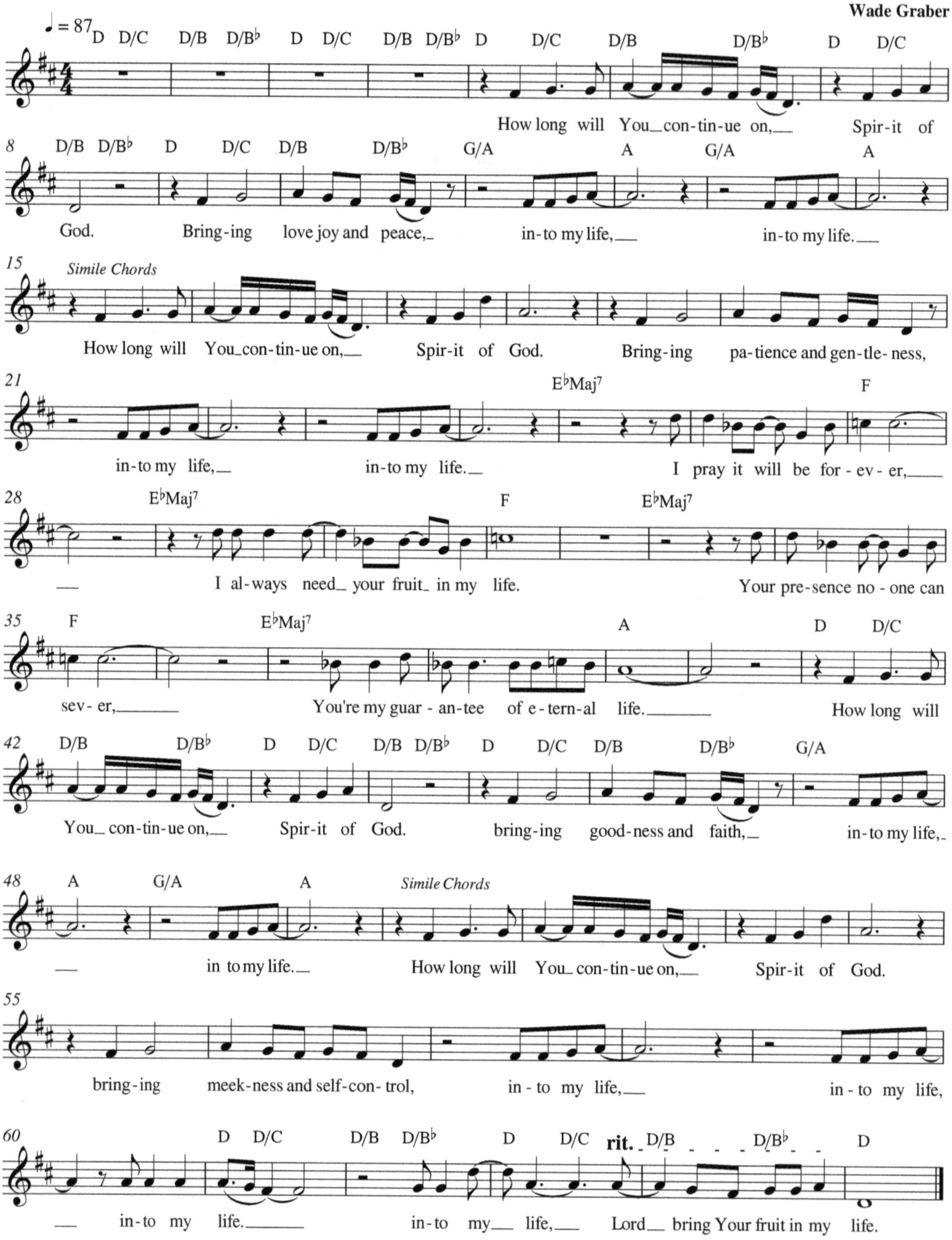


© 2010 Wade Graber/Graber Ministries

# Keep on Being Filled

*Original music and lyrics by:*
**Gary Graber**
*New lyrics by:*
**Wade C. Graber**

Jesus Christ is Lord,— His Spirit's in me. — Internal fountain,— springing up_ in me.— And I__keep on being filled, yes I__keep on being filled,_ Oh I__keep on be-ing filled_____ with the Lord.__ Endless source of life,— welling up in me,— filled to_ over-flow, pour-ing out_ of me.__ And I___keep on being filled,— yes I___keep on being filled,_ Oh I___keep on be-ing filled_____ with the Lord._____ The bi-ble doesn't stop with sal-va-tion. Jesus says, "Go and sin_ no more."_____

47 There is more_ like be-ing filled with the Spir - it. so let Him dwell, in your heart,

53 let Him reign, in your life_ let Him flow._____ Don't ne-glect God's word,

60 ___ or try to change His plan, ex - per - ience His Spir-it, o-ver and o-ver a-

66 - gain. Keep on_ be-ing filled, Keep on_ be-ing filled, oh____ keep on be - ing filled___

73 ___ with the Lord.____ with His Spir - it,_____ with His Spir - it,_____

# Holy Spirit, Intercede

Wade Graber

**Reflective** ♩ = 53

C  F² C  F² Dm  G  C  F/G  G

C  F²  C  F²  Dm  G

On-ly Your Spir-it can pray_____ what-ev-er we can - not say,_ Ho-ly Spir - it in-ter

C  F/G  G  C  F²  C  F²  Dm

cede._____ When we can't find the word may it in heav - en_____ be heard,_ Ho-ly Spir-

G  C  C  G/B  Am  Em  Am  Em

- it in -ter- cede. We are frail,_ help us in our weak - ness,_

Am  Em  Am  Em  Dm

we don't know what to_____ pray,_ please groan what we can't_ speak,_ Ho - ly Spir-
please pray the Fath - ers_____ will,_

G  C  F/G  G  C  F²  C

- it in -ter cede. On-ly Your Spir - it can pray_____ what-ev-er we can - not say,

F²  Dm  G  C  F/G  G  C  F²

_ Ho - ly Spir - it in-ter- cede._____ When we can't find the word, may it in

C  F²  Dm  G  C  G/A  *cresc.* A

heav - en_____ be heard,_ Ho-ly Spir - it in-ter- cede.

On-ly Your Spir- it can pray_____ what-ev-er we can - not say, Ho-ly Spir - it inter

cede._____ When we can't find the word, may it in heav - en_____ be heard,_ Ho-ly Spir-

- it inter- cede._____ Ho - ly Spir - it inter- cede._____

Ho - ly Spir - it inter- cede._____

# You Live in Me

Wade Graber

♩ = 61

G    GM7    C/G    D/G    G    GM7    C/G    D/G    *p*

You live in me,

**9** G    GM7    C/G    D/G    G

You live in me, Ho-ly Spir-it You live in me. You live in me, You live in

**14** GM7    C/G    D/G    C    G/B    C    D G/B

me, Ho-ly Spir-it You live in me. My bo-dy is Your tem-ple You live deep in side, it

**19** C    G/B    Am    *cresc.*    Dsus    D    *mf* G

is Your Ho-ly dwell-ing, the place where You re - side. You live in me, You live in

**24** GM7    C/G    D/G    G    GM7

me, Ho-ly Spir-it You live in me. You live in me, You live in me, Ho-ly

**29** C/G    D/G    C    G/B    C    D G/B

Spir-it You live in me. My bo-dy is Your tem-ple You live deep in-side it

**33** C    G/B    Am    Dsus    Ebsus    Eb    *f*

is Your ho-ly dwell-ing, the place where You re - side. You live in me,

2

You live in me, Holy Spirit You live in me. You live in me, You live in

me, Holy Spirit You live in me. My body is Your temple, You live deep inside, it

is Your Holy dwelling, the place where You reside. You live in me, You live in

me, Holy Spirit You live in me. You live in me, You live in

me, Holy Spirit You live in me. You live in me.

# Speak to Me

Words and Music:
Stephen Butler/Wade Graber

♩=65

**Voice** — D | G | D | F#m7 | Bm7

Speak Ho-ly Spir - it, in all Your ma-ny ways I want to hear Your voice to - night, I

**Voice** — Em7 | C2 | D | G | A | Bm

want to give You praise. Speak Ho-ly Spir - it, Draw me to Your face I

**Voice** — G9 | D/F# | Em7 | A7 | D | Asus A

want to hear the Word of God be - fore I leave this place.

**Voice** — D mf | F#m7 | G | Asus A | D | F#m7

Ho - ly Spir - it Speak to me Ho - ly Spir - it Come and

**Voice** — G | Asus A | Bm7 f | F#m7 | G9 | D9/F#

Speak to me Ho-ly Spir - it Speak to me I

**2nd time to CODA ⊕**

**Voice** — Em7 | Asus A | D | G/A D mf

want to hear Your voice. Speak to me Je - sus I

**Voice** — G | D | F#m7 | Bm7

want to know Your way. I know that You're a might - y God would You

*21* Em⁷  C² D  G A Bm

Voice

teach me how to pray? Speak to me Je - sus and I will fol - low You If You

*24* G  D/F♯  Em A D  D Asus A

Voice

lead me to a - noth - er world You will see me through!

**CODA**

*27* D  A♭/B♭  E♭ *f* Gm⁷  A♭  B♭sus B♭

Voice

voice.  Ho-ly Spir - it  Speak to me

*30* E♭ Gm⁷  A♭  B♭sus B♭ E♭ *ff* Gm⁷

Voice

Ho-ly Spir - it Come and Speak to me  Ho-ly Spir - it

*33* A♭9  Gm⁷sus⁶ Gm⁷ A♭  B♭sus B♭ E♭ B♭/D Cm⁷

Voice

Speak to me  I want to hear Your voice, I

*36* Fm⁷  B♭sus B♭ Cm⁷  E♭ *mp*

Voice

want to hear Your voice, I

*38* Fm⁷ **rit.** B♭sus B♭ E♭ Gm A♭ E♭/G Fm B♭sus B♭ E♭ **rall.**

Voice

want to hear Your voice.